I AM THE WOUNDED VICTIM OF A SUICIDE BOMBER

Mizan Series

The Mizan Series supports the central mission of the Mizan Project, a digital initiative to encourage informed public discourse and interdisciplinary scholarship on the history, culture, and religion of Muslim societies and civilizations.

www.mizanproject.org

Also in the Mizan Series

Muslim Superheroes: Comics, Islam, and Representation,
edited by A. David Lewis and Martin Lund

Muslims and US Politics Today: A Defining Moment
edited by Mohammad Hassan Khalil

The End of Middle East History and Other Conjectures
by Richard W. Bulliet

Deconstructing Islamic Studies
edited by Majid Daneshgar and Aaron W. Hughes

Muslims in the Movies: A Global Anthology
edited by Kristian Petersen

I AM THE WOUNDED VICTIM OF A SUICIDE BOMBER

A Book of Poems

FAZEL AHAD AHADI

TRANSLATED BY
POUNEH SHABANI-JADIDI AND PATRICIA J. HIGGINS

FOREWORD BY NILE GREEN

Ilex Project
Boston, Massachusetts

Distributed by Harvard University Press
Cambridge, Massachusetts and London, England

I Am the Wounded Victim of a Suicide Bomber: A Book of Poems
by Fazel Ahad Ahadi

Originally published in Kabul, Afghanistan by Goruh-e Farhangi-ye Hamzabanan in 2023.

Published in the United States by Ilex Project, an imprint of New Alexandria Foundation,
84 Revere Street, Boston, MA 02114 .
cd@ilexfoundation.org

Distributed by Harvard University Press, Cambridge, MA and London

Printed by Gasch Printing, 1780 Crossroads Drive, Odenton, MD 21113.
info@gaschprinting.com

EU GPSR Authorized Representative: LOGOS EUROPE,
9 rue Nicolas Poussin, 17000, La Rochelle, France.
Contact@logoseurope.eu

Production editor: Christopher Dadian
Cover design: Joni Godlove
Printed in the United States of America

Cover Image: The Salsal Buddha Statue in Bamiyan. Photo by Ali Omid, journalist and photographer, 2007.

Library of Congress Cataloging-in-Publication data is available from the Library of Congress at https://lccn.loc.gov/

ISBN 9780674303270

CONTENTS

Foreword

Nile Green

HISTORY AND LITERATURE, poetry and politics, violence and the arts, all have been intimately and brutally bound together in modern Afghanistan. On Christmas Eve 1979, while the Western world was distracted, the Soviet Union invaded Afghanistan, setting in motion a cycle of international wars and internal conflicts that would continue for over four decades. Two months after Soviet tanks crossed the border, Fazel Ahad Ahadi was born in the Panjshir Valley, north of Kabul. Between spring 1980 and summer 1985 this area became the focus of some of the heaviest fighting of the decade as the Soviets tried to take the strategic valley from the guerilla force led by Ahmad Shah Massoud. Ahadi grew up during those and following years, turning twelve as resistance to the Soviets descended into a still more destructive civil war among rival factions of mujahidin. The divisions and misdeeds of these 'holy warriors' paved the way in turn for the ascent of a new group of fighters, dubbed Taliban, or 'students,' through their origins in the makeshift madrasa schools of Pakistan's refugee camps. Ahadi was sixteen when the Taliban first came to power in 1996.

By the time the Taliban were ousted – at least from Kabul and the other major cities – by an American-led alliance in December 2001, Ahadi was about to turn twenty-one. But after just four years of peace and optimism, in 2005, urban Afghanistan became home to a new form of violence: suicide bombing. Invented in Sri Lanka during its vicious civil war, then massively expanded in the Iraq conflict of the early 2000s, suicide bombing found a new home in Afghanistan. The first instance on Afghan soil had occurred back in September 2001, when, just days before their assault on the United States, al-Qaeda (which had been founded during the anti-Soviet jihad) dispatched two suicide bombers to assassinate the aforementioned Ahmad Shah Massoud. This portent of future horrors took place in Ahadi's home region of Panjshir. It was merely a taste of what was to come: between 2005 and 2006, the number of suicide bombings in Afghanistan would increase more than fivefold then grow even more over the next fifteen years till the Taliban's return to power in 2021.

Throughout these four decades of war and civil conflict, poetry retained a strikingly prevalent position in Afghan society, whether in Persian (the language in which Ahadi writes), Pashto, or minority languages such as Uzbek and Balochi. This is partly a matter of literary tradition: the short story and novel were latecomers to Afghanistan, emerging only around 1920, and then mainly by way of short stories in Persian. Theater has an even briefer history and one, like the short story and novel, partly bound up with the ideologies and institutions of Soviet-supported Afghan socialists, who cultivated these media as vehicles for a new literature of social realism intended to criticize Afghanistan's social, religious, and cultural heritage. By contrast, poetry not only has a much longer history in Afghanistan. It has also been used as a medium to explore a far broader spectrum of philosophical, moral, and political positions than drama or prose. From lengthy narrative and didactic modes to classical lyrical forms and modern variations of free verse inspired by European and Iranian poets alike, Afghan poets have worked in a wide variety of genres.

However, the reasons for the continued prominence of poetry in modern Afghanistan as compared to, say, the English-speaking world, are not only a matter of the continuation of a literary culture that has long valorized verse, prosody, and meter over plain or even embellished prose. The reasons are also entrenched in the living realities of Afghan society. Despite various successive and opposing attempts to expand education in Afghanistan, attempts which have alternated from the secular nationalists of the 1970s to the communists of the 1980s, the Taliban of the 1990s, and the NGOs of the 2000s, the country's literacy rate has remained stubbornly low. According to the UNESCO Institute for Statistics, just before the Soviets invaded in 1979 adult male basic literacy stood at around 30%. By the time of the US withdrawal in 2021, it had still reached only 52%. The figures for adult female literacy are far lower still: 5% in 1979 and 23% in 2021. These statistics offer us a socio-literary snapshot of Fazel Ahad Ahadi's lifetime in Afghanistan before he left his homeland in 2022 after the Taliban returned to power.

Such limited literacy has also meant that poetry has been and continues to be a medium accessible to women as well as men, both as authors and listeners (if not necessarily as writers and readers). Female participation dates right back to "the woman poet Rabia" invoked in one of Ahadi's poems who composed Persian poems in tenth-century Balkh. It was around that time, and in the Khurasan region that stretches across what is today northern Afghanistan, eastern Iran, and southern Uzbekistan, that poetry first began to be written and preserved in the Persian language. Together with Balkh, another famous early literary cradle of Persian poetry was the capital of the Samanid dynasty in Bukhara (now in Uzbekistan). This primordial literary geography is evoked by Ahadi's opening poem in this collection in the lines,

زاده‌ی بلخ و بخارایم، یلِ سامانی‌ام

My birthplace, Balkh and Bukhara;
I'm a Samanid hero.

In the pages that follow, subsequent poems summon other key sites of Afghan literary history, such as Ghazni – the home of Sana'i, who died between 1131 and 1141 – and Balkh (or Vakhsh), where Jalal al-Din Rumi was born in the year 1207. Hence, we read of

کشمش از غزنی برایت تحفه، توت از پنجشیر
یک کمی از شهر مولانا نبات آورده‌ام

Raisins from Ghazni
and mulberries from Panjshir
as souvenirs for you,
I've brought
a bit of sugar crystal
from Rumi's hometown.

Here Ahadi combines motifs from literary geography with the vivid living fruits of the land, setting the famous mulberries of his home Panjshir region with the *nabat*, or sugar crystal, of Rumi's hometown – a substance associated with the sweet rapture of mystical experience. But whereas the poetry of Sana'i and Rumi expressed the theology and ecstasy of Sufi Islam, the poet Ahadi most frequently invokes is Ferdowsi, who celebrated heroic battles in his epic *Shahnameh* (Book of Kings), composed as he traipsed in search of patronage between the courts of the Samanids and their Ghaznavid successors.

رهنمایم بوعلی، تاریخ من شهنامه است
لحن و صوت و چامه و نظم و سرودم؛ پارسی ست

My guide, Avicenna;
my history, *Shahnameh*.
My tone, voice, melody,
and poems are Persian

Like the life of Ferdowsi himself – whose body, tradition tells, was carried out of the western gate of his hometown of Tus just as the sultan's courier rode through the eastern gate with the poet's long-awaited prize of gold – the martial and romantic stories he recounted in his *Shahnameh* point to the close early ties between Persian literature and the courts of warrior-kings. Even mystics like Sana'i and Rumi relied on the patronage of sultans. Albeit in different ways, literature and state remained no less closely entwined in twentieth-century Afghanistan. As the country experimented with different forms of modernization – nationalist, socialist, Islamist – new institutions were founded to direct literary production to serve the dominant ideology of the day. The first of these was the Kabul Literary Society (Anjoman-e adabi-e Kabol), which was established in 1930 to promote a modern, national literature under the close scrutiny of government ministers. After initially supporting Persian, by the late 1930s a shift in cultural nationalist policy saw ministers try to replace Persian with Pashto as the country's official language, prompting the Kabul Literary Society to be disbanded and replaced in 1940 by the Pashto Society (Pashto tolana).

Despite this attempt to overturn a millennium of literary history, Persian continued to remain the primary language of literature, education, and governance, even as nationalist officials and opposition communists sought to promote Pashto as alternatively the language of the nation or the masses. A case in point is Nur Muhammad Taraki (1917–79), who, before his eighteen-month rule of terror, had been a journalist and novelist who made his name in 1957 with the Pashto novel, *Da Bang musafiri* (The Journey of Bang), which voiced a Marxist critique of rural Afghan customs. After Taraki was murdered and replaced by members of a rival communist faction, the ensuing arrival of the Soviets saw the founding in 1980 of the Writers Union of Afghanistan, which, as part of the apparatus of the ruling People's Democratic Party and their Soviet sponsors, directed Afghan authors to write, whether in Persian and Pashto, in tune with 'progressive' Marxist precepts. After the Soviet withdrawal of 1989, the Writers Union collapsed, just in time for the first period of Taliban rule to usher in another cultural revolution between 1996 and 2001. Among the first literary victims of the Taliban's Ministry for the Propagation of Virtue and the Prevention of Vice were the television dramas and radio programs which, under Soviet tutelage, had served as vehicles for social engineering and the making of the new Afghan woman. For all that, Afghan television and especially radio had served as vital outlets for artistic creativity.

Throughout these tumultuous changes, poetry remained the most stalwart medium of Afghan cultural life. Poetry required no patronage, nor was it even necessary to be literate to engage with it, since recitation and memorization remained vital cultural practices. And when poems did appear in published form, they were often printed in cheap and cheerful pamphlets that could be read aloud, shared, committed to memory, and if necessary, hidden away.

In her memoir of reporting from Afghanistan between 2006 and 2013, the Indian journalist Taran Khan gives an evocative description of the stalls selling such poetry booklets in the Koh-e Asma'i neighborhood of Kabul. "Some stalls were basic and exposed to gusts of wind that deposited dust on their stock," she writes; "others were equipped with computers and heating. Some of the stalls had been painted brightly, and the splashy colours appeared as a contrast against the adobe mud houses that clustered above... the labyrinth of narrow book-lined gullies."[1] Koh-e Asma'i is just one of many literary marketplaces that have kept poetry alive over the past forty years.

Not that writing (or even selling) poetry was ever without risk in modern Afghanistan. Even though one of poetry's great assets as a medium of public expression is its ambiguity, allowing authors the plausible deniability of metaphors and symbols that could be read as contemporary critiques or classical allusions, many prominent poets have found themselves nonetheless forced into exile. Mahmud Tarzi (1865–1933), arguably the founder of modern Afghan literature, was raised in Ottoman Syria with his banished father (and fellow poet) before his triumphant return to Kabul (and high government office) ended in his own exile to Istanbul, where he died. The mid-twentieth century saw other leading literary figures, such as Khalilullah Khalili (1909–87), Baha al-Din Majruh (1928–88), and Abd al-Rahman Pazhwak (1919–95), fall foul of nationalist or communist governments, spending time in prison or in exile. Majruh was assassinated by mujahidin in the Pakistani city of Peshawar.

Echoing these earlier literary exiles, and millions of unsung refugees, Ahadi writes,

بنگر چه‌گونه بی سر و بی پا و تن شدیم
بی‌خانمان و دربه در و بی‌وطن شدیم

Look how we lost our head,
our feet, and our body;
How we became displaced,
homeless, and nationless.

For a thousand years, poets writing in Persian have alternated between the registers of historicity and transcendence, between the physically rooted and

1 Taran N. Khan, *Shadow City: A Woman Walks Kabul* (London: Vintage, 2019), 49.

the mystically abstract. These registers echo too through Ahadi's verses, some of which evoke the urban and rural landscapes of his homeland, while others conjure the classical imagery of mirrors, gazes, madness, idol-temples, and "the ascension of compassion." Ahadi self-consciously writes within a tradition with whose masters his poems are in dialogue, both implicitly and explicitly. Calling across space and time to medieval and modern poets who lived in what are today India and Iran, he declares,

مکتبم اقبال و بیدل، درس من فردوسی است
تکیه گاهم حضرت سعدی وجودم؛ پارسی ست

My school, Iqbal and Bedil;
my lesson, Ferdowsi.
My pillar of support, Sa'di;
my being is Persian.

Other poems reach beyond history to the spacetime of myth, to the heroic age depicted by the medieval Ferdowsi in his tales of Khosrow and Shirin, Rostam and Sohrab, and in even more recent times by Siavash Kasra'i, whose 1959 epic *Arash-e kamangir* (Arash the Archer) retold the legend of Arash as a socialist parable of Iranian liberation from European imperialism. (Kasra'i later resided in Kabul during its decade of communist rule.) Then there are those poems in which Ahadi enters the mythosphere of Muslim scripture and ceremony, invoking the Quranic archetypes of Joseph and Abraham, and the rituals that commemorate the martyrdom of the Prophet's grandson Hossein at Karbala. Then, turning the page, we are suddenly brought back to Afghanistan's here-and-now. There is a panegyric to Qahar Asi (1956–94), a fellow Panjshiri poet who in such works as *Az jazira-ye khun* (From the Island of Blood) addressed the violence of the civil war in which he would himself die during a mujahidin rocket attack on Kabul.

Bringing us to more recent times, another of Ahadi's poems serves as a furious dirge to female victims of such violence:

موی کسی دیدی که قیچی خورد در تهران؟
فرخنده را وقتی که در دادند، در کابل

در کاج دهها دختر مظلوم را کشتند
تابوت را دست پدر دادند، در کابل

Did you see
when hair was shorn in Tehran?

When they set fire
on Farkhondeh in Kabul?

Tens of innocent girls
killed in Kaj School.
Coffins were handed
to fathers in Kabul.

In these lines Ahadi commemorates Farkhondeh Malikzad, a young woman who in 2015 was beaten to death then burned by a mob in Kabul after rumors spread that she worked with the Americans and had burned the Quran, and the forty-six girls killed in a suicide bombing in September 2022 at the Kaj education center in Kabul, attended by children of the Hazara Shiʿi minority.

"History, Stephen said, is a nightmare from which I am trying to awake." So runs the famous line of James Joyce's *Ulysses* voiced by the author's alter ego, Stephen Dedalus. Few peoples in modern times have been forced to live through the nightmare of history for as long as the inhabitants of Afghanistan. The poems of Fazel Ahad Ahadi offer testimony to the suffering caused by countless killers of varied backgrounds and competing causes who "have robbed the sun / from the sky of my nation." And yet, his verses also offer the solace of transcending present horrors – of entering the alternative reality offered by the literary heritage of Persian:

از دوره‌های شاد جوانی و تازه‌گی
افسانه و حکایت و ضرب‌المثل بگو

Tell me of happy times,
of youth, and of bloom.
Tell me of myths,
of tales, and of proverbs.

Here Ahadi reminds us why poetry has always remained a vital companion through the cruel vicissitudes of Afghanistan's history.

Further Reading

Ahmadi, Wali. 2008. *Modern Persian Literature in Afghanistan: Anomalous Visions of History and Form*. London: Routledge.

Fani, Aria. 2024. *Reading Across Borders: Afghans, Iranians, and Literary Nationalism*. Austin: University of Texas Press.

Green, Nile and Nushin Arbabzadah, eds. 2012. *Afghanistan in Ink: Literature Between Diaspora and Nation*. New York: Columbia University Press.

Green, Nile, ed. 2017. *Afghanistan's Islam: From Conversion to the Taliban*. Berkeley: University of California Press. Open Access: https://www.ucpress.edu/read/books/afghanistans-islam

Khalili, Khalilullah. 2012. *Memoirs of Khalilullah Khalili: An Afghan Philosopher Poet*. Edited and translated by Afzal Nasiri and Marie Khalili. Virginia: Afzal Nasiri and Marie Khalili.

1

Who am I?
You, better than others,
know me.
I'm from Badakhshan and Herat,
a citizen of Khatlon.

I'm a bright bolt of lightning
in the sky of darkness.
My birthplace, Balkh and Bukhara;
I'm a Samanid champion.

I'm the son of Rostam,
Sohrab and Kay Qobad.
I'm of the Sassanid race,
jewel and seed.

Ardeshir Babakan
has taught me freedom.
I'm of the lineage of Khosrow,
of royal ancestry.

From my father,
I've inherited honor and valor.
No one could ever defeat me,
nor will you.

Barbad's song
has caressed my heart.
I'm of the Aryans,
descendant of kings.

I follow the way of Saman,
of Abu Muslim.
I'm the savior
in every stormy moment and time.

Our culture, our history,
you know all so well.
I'm a mirror
reflecting humanity for all.

I'm Tajik, Tajik indeed.
I'm a true-blooded Tajik.
I fear you not;
with what do you frighten me?

2

Did you see how easily
they sold our homeland?
How they sold this ancient, old land?

Forever they shut
our protesting mouths.
They sold the words
from our lips.

It's hard to believe;
how shall I tell you?
From martyrs' graves,
they sold the shrouds.

Anywhere they entered
the foreigners' houses,
like prostitutes,
they sold their own bodies.

Curse upon this trade
and their foolish minds.
For they even sold the body,
piece by piece.

What good now
to protect its borders,
when they've sold its mountains,
its plains, and its meadows?

3

Do not believe in my stature,
tall and firm;
I am the wounded victim
of a suicide bomber.

Like fissures of wounds
on the body,
I am the blood plasma
oozing from the flesh of the ill.

Trapped in a cage
my whole life,
I am the broken wings
of a canary.

Banished from our cities
and towns,
I am the one
long fleeing this city
of yours.

I am a lump
caught in the throat;
may the day come
that you set me free.

Now, if you may,
let me be,
as I am incurable pain
and infectious disease.

I've grown accustomed
to the fall;
I am the never-bloomed buds
of spring.

Do not test my strength,
nor my patience;
I am the wounded victim
of a suicide bomber.

4

Go to Kufa no more;
the Karbala battleground is here.
All the events, the deaths,
the incidents are here.

See how my homeland is drowned,
sunken in blood.
Everywhere I look,
mourning and wailing are here.

How can I hold my pain,
my sorrow in my heart?
Sorrow pulling me
toward collapse is here.

Come and see
the Karbala battle again.
Headless, limbless,
lifeless Hossein is here.

I shall not go back
to the wrecked boat.
The headless, lifeless captain is here.

How, with what hope,
shall I love my homeland?
A thousand evils,
a hundred impieties and injustices are here.

For this land of mine,
no longer is there hope or desire.
Only the one who has gone
into seclusion is here.

5

I'm the notebook pages
gone with every wind.

I'm the prey
gone on its own to the hunter.

O Cameleer,
let Jacob know!
I'm Joseph,
forgotten by the caravan.

You're a city like Kabul,
drowned in blood.
I've gone through cruelty,
ignorance, and injustice.

My every turret, every nook,
sunken in the dust.
I'm a wall with no base,
and no foundation.

No crime have I done
to be taken to the gallows.
I've gone to the executioner
on my own two feet.

I'm yellowed with age,
pages crumpled with use.
I'm torn to pieces.
I've gone wherever
the wind has driven me.

6

Opportunities finally emerged,
but time was gone.
Hope was off the table,
bread was gone.

The season of love finally arrived,
but the season of autumn befell.
Gusts of wind began,
home was gone.

I'm the lost Joseph,
fallen into the well.
Before I was pulled out,
the caravan was gone.

By day, my refuge
was the shadow of the wall.
The walls were destroyed,
the shade was gone.

Empty-handed, how shall I handle
the vicious hyenas?
One by one, arrows had missed,
until the bow was gone.

7

We knew our heart's blood
as we did food.
We knew only tears;
we knew only pain.

We are the oppressed,
the wronged children of time.
It's a shame that
we knew everyone's pain.

Just pain and sorrow,
just fire and fear.
We knew neither joy
nor laughter.

Cries and shouts
stuck in our throats.
We knew guns
as walking sticks.

Fresh out of the kiln,
we are the hardest.
We knew every event
as a disaster.

We killed, we maimed,
we jailed, yet in the end,
we knew everyone's blood
as we did henna.

We endured pain
but made no sound.
We knew our heart's patience
as a cure.

Never seen in the pages of history
such an event.
By God, we knew the swearing in
of two kings on one day.

8

I'm a son of Balkh, Sogdiana,
and Samangan, still.
I'm a brave warrior
of Khorasan, still.

The blood of Khosrow Parviz
flows in my veins.
I'm an epic hero
of the Sassanid era, still.

Rostam is not dead;
Arash and Sohrab are alive.
I'm the legends
of the golden age, still.

Wherever Kaveh's flag
is raised, that's me.
I'm a champion
of the royal era, still.

My body from Kabul,
my soul from Bukhara.
I'm a soldier
of the Samanid era, still.

Though my body's wounds
are fresh,
I'm smiling at moments
in bewilderment, still.

My stature not shaken
by the humble winds,
I'm a savior from the pain
of stormy times, still.

So long as Abu Muslim
is the tale's hero, so am I.
I'm neither dead,
nor am I the final tale, still.

The roof of the world
is the land I rule.
I'm a proud man
of Badakhshan, still.

Time might have drawn
a border between us; yet,
I'm from Khujand, Mashhad,
and Khatlon, still.

I'm from Herat, and you,
from Bukhara and Isfahan.
I know you,
but you don't know me, still.

However little I share
in all such traits,
I'm a proud child
of Keraman, still.

9

I seem fine,
yet my mind and soul
are unwell.

My body,
head to toe,
has a fever;
my spirit is unwell.

I've no strength
to talk,
after this.
I've been punched in the face;
my mouth is unwell.

Believe not my smiling face
and apparent joy.
Take my word,
every joint in my bones is unwell.

After this,
I have no desire
to recite a love poem.
For it's days
that my spirit and mood are unwell.

My nest has been ruined
by gusts of wind.
After this,
the state of my home is unwell.

10

Shame on you;
the shirt from this body,
sell not.
Each part and member
of this body,
sell not.

Though the passions
of the body
concern me not,
it's full of pain and sorrow;

this homeland,
sell not.

This earth is filled
with martyrs' blood.
Beware!
The shroud from every grave
of the dead,
sell not.

If this land
is your mother's abode,
the plain and meadows,
sell not.

Make kohl with dust
of the homeland and apply.
Flowers have bloomed
in the garden;
the pasture, sell not.

Weave a cord
with the thread of kindness.
Make a chain;
the cord, sell not.

If you don't cut the cord
of this trade,
you may sell yourselves;
me, sell not!

11

Like a house in ruins,
I've tumbled down.
From head to trunk to feet,
I've tumbled down.

For days they threw stones
at my wings.

From the nest like a dove,
I've tumbled down.

Whosoever sees me,
laughs at my state.
Like a mad man,
I've tumbled down.

No place have I got
in my beloved's heart.
Yet from the stranger's eye,
I've tumbled down.

Like a withered flowering vine,
no longer clinging to the wall,
from the door and walls of the house,
I've tumbled down.

12

What uncultured beings
we are dealing with!
Under enemy torment
and vicious conduct,
we've fallen.

Their ominous faces
looked non-human.
In the claws of old vultures
and hyenas,
we've been trapped.

No sign of humanity
in their thoughts.
In the clutches of hired mercenaries,
we've been caught.

No weapon in our hands,
save the pen.
In what a shape

and how humiliated,
we've fallen!

They broke branches;
they burned houses and gardens.
Onto thirsty land and desert,
we've fallen.

One day, their massive rancor
shall come to an end.
No matter their liking,
we'll be blessed.

The day of resolve
and revenge
will come.
For now,
in the claws of the jackal,
we're helpless.

13

When will it be
that we ask for cotton gauze
and coffins no more?
That after every incident,
we ask for gunpowder no more?

That my countrymen's legs
will no longer be severed?
That we'll ask for boots
for prosthetic legs no more?

That for every young branch
full of fruit,
for every green flower stem,
we'll ask for an ax
from the divine world no more?

That Joseph won't be thrown
to the bottom of the well

by his brothers?
When will it be
that we ask for a ditch
or some arid land no more?

That we no longer search
high and low for a crumb?
That by every road,
we ask for a morsel
of food no more?

That war will be over
and peace arrive here?
When will it be
that we ask for cotton gauze
and coffins no more?

14

How easily these dealers
sold bodies and souls.
Dignity, pride, honor,
and conscience, they sold.

For status, power,
position, and glory.
Alas, how easily they sold
their whole being, then and now.

Blood money rights
for our thousands of martyrs,
how easily and how cheaply
were sold by these scoundrels.

Nothing did they do
but make deals.
For their own survival,
they even sold their faith.

We're still alive,
yet our rights and dues,

they sold in secret,
concealed, and hidden.

No respect did they have
for bread and butter.
They ate the bread, yet
bit the hand that fed them.

For what we brought upon ourselves,
there was no pain and no remedy.
Alas, what a shame
that they sold humanity!

If they sold their bodies and souls,
it pains me not.
That they sold the good name
of Khorasan, that pains me so!

15

On a clear day,
we bear the rain.
We bear the cruelty
of our era's tyranny.

So long as the devil
hasn't halted the war,
we bear Satan's work
without regard.

So long as the flag
of liberty is not waving,
we bear the chain
and bludgeon of jail.

So long as the curtain
concealing the truth
hasn't been drawn back,
we bear the hidden secret
day by day.

So long as the lily
and the marigold
haven't bloomed,
we bear the winter
cold and its snow.

We wait until the climate
in the country improves.
We bear the state
and the manner of the crisis.

So long as blood rains
from the map of my homeland,
we bear the pain
and the wail of Khurasan.

16

How sad a state,
how hard a test it was.
No chance of peace for my tears;
no check on the lump in my throat.

She smiled sweetly
when I glanced at her.
In a rather shabby dress,
barely a teen she was.

She stood behind the restaurant window,
packages of gum in her hand.
From the diner's doorway,
her eyes looked for a scrap of bread.

A load of pain on her shoulders,
a world of tears in her eyes.
In her tight throat I saw
an infinity of sorrow and sadness.

When I asked about her past,
she told her story bit by bit.

"In providing us bread and butter,
my father was quite a hero.

All under one roof,
life was getting better day by day.
So that we be in need of no one,
he was like a parasol.

My father left and never returned,
the victim of a suicide bombing.
All the world's sorrow rained down
on our home,
whatever was in the sky."

Tears flowed through her black lashes
onto the bosom of the earth.
Ah ... How strange,
how full of tragedy
that moment was.

Hearing her story,
I grew numb,
and in the end,
I had neither strength
in my legs,
nor power of expression.

Whatever money
I had in my pocket,
I poured into her lap.
A wave of a smiles
appeared on her lips
like celestial light.

Pouring out all the sorrow
and grief from my heart,
I wept for an hour,
till my last breath and strength.

Suddenly the lump
in my throat

exploded like a bomb.
How sad a state,
how hard a test it was.

17

They've broken my pride,
dignity, and glory here.
They've broken my wall,
ceiling, roof, and door.

I'm like the lone poplar tree
in the corner of the garden.
They've broken the golden branches
surrounding me.

Hold my hand
and teach me valor,
O Abraham!
This idolatrous tribe
of infidels
has broken my ax.

I wish to live
with my head up high.
Yet, they've broken
my hands and feet,
and my head, too.

I wished to fly
in the space of love.
But see how they have
broken my wings.

18

A mother awaits
the return of her son,
once again.

A son awaits
the return of his father,
once again.

A child gazes
at the image of his father.
A sister awaits word,
once again.

Eyes glued
to the window
at times.
Staring dazed
at the door
once again.

In sorrow
for his son,
his body has bent.
The father holding his back
with both hands,
once again.

The tie uniting the hands
of the lovers has dropped.
Like newlyweds,
they should be on a journey,
once again.

The table of grave diggers
full of good food.
Smiling, the shroud maker
hopes for success,
once again.

Our homeland's walls and doors
have been bloodied,
once again.
Look at its people,
headless, legless, bodyless,
once again.

19

Life has remained
in a halo of uncertainty.
It's our foot that's caught
in the trap, only.

In the speech and talk
of my country's people,
curses and swear words
have remained, only.

No doubt do I live
in a land where
the dignity of humanity
has remained in word, only.

No place for maturity
in our eyes anymore.
Our beliefs and thoughts
have remained crude, only.

Our eyes opened to the sound
of weeping every moment.
The bitter taste of enmity
has remained in our mouth, only.

I'm dead here, yet
looking for my soul.
My body has remained
at the foot of gallows, only.

20

With blistered feet,
I must leave.
With patience and forbearance,
I must leave.

That I may not be lost
in my homeland's dust,

following this caravan,
I must leave.

Life's injustice
has tied my feet; yet,
with this bond and this chain,
I must leave.

Were I to wish
to take a breath
in peace and calm,
this disaster and oppression
I must leave.

That I not be the log
in this era's fire,
at this time and this chance,
I must leave.

21

No excuse
to go back again,
no hope for my home
to go back again.

Desire for your poetry
is long gone from my mind.
No song have I left
to go back again.

Heart and mind
at peace since leaving.
No desire for that land
to go back again.

No companion,
no true friend,
have I in this era
to go back again.

No one to put his head
on my shoulder,
from the heart of his heart,
to go back again.

22

Pray for me,
for I have hard days ahead.
Ask God for refuge,
for I have hard days ahead.

Disaster in ambush
surrounds us these days.
Come, save me from disaster,
for I have hard days ahead.

Nothing do I wish
from you but prayer, my love!
Pay heed to my words,
for I have hard days ahead.

Midnight prayers
might be granted.
Pray along with me,
for I have hard days ahead.

Did you not say that
you will never forget
to pray for me?
Come, keep your promise,
for I have hard days ahead.

You're getting farther from me
in this strangeness.
Get to know it,
for I have hard days ahead.

23

Winter snow and ice,
cold, all so different.
Crime and sin,
corner of jail, all so different.

Wolves in ambush,
the desert all silent.
Mountain, valley,
"hey, hey" of shepherds,
all so different.

Our foe,
foe no more;
our friend,
friend no more.
War and dispute,
fistfight, all so different.

What can I say
about the dire state
of the Kunduz people?
Balkh, the most ruined,
Badakhshan, all so different.

Takhar's peace
upset these days.
Bangi turned to ruins,
Kalafgan, all so different.

Roars "God is Great"
from Shamali silenced.
Paryan in chaos,
Parwan, all so different.

Air is freezing
in Pol-e-Khomri.
What can I say
about Khwaja and Jelga?
All of Baghlan, all so different.

The state of the hearts
of Ghazni people unknown.
Ghor, Kunar, Logar,
Laghman, all so different.

Zabul, city of rage
and pain.
Shah Joy, Qalat, Otghar,
Mizan, all so different.

Startled by Herat,
city full of pain.
Adraskan, ruined,
Gulran, all so different.

Herat River red
with your blood.
Heavy with sorrow,
Gulran, all so different.

Almar and Qaramqol,
city full of sorrow.
Kharwar, isolated,
Zadran, all so different.

Samangan and Sar-e Pol,
no exception.
Qarqin, all ruined,
Sheberghan, all so different.

People of the south,
weeping blood.
Urgun, Surobi,
Mata Khan, all so different.

Who can I tell
about your fire and smoke,
O Kabul?
Your day is dark,
your refuge, all so different.

Humans are said
to all be members
of one body.
This saying seems a lie;
humans, all so different.

Full of pain,
full of sorrow
is my home.
Every hour,
every moment,
Keraman, all so different.

O poor homeland
of mine,
drowning in blood!
Your pain
has filled my soul;
the cure, all so different.

24

Where's the one
who would fight for freedom,
flag in hand, and on lips,
the chant of freedom?

Where's the one
who, for the sake of home,
would march toward victory,
in step with freedom?

I'm captive of the foe here,
captive only of myself.
Where's the spiritual master
and the guide to freedom?

Voice stuck
in the throat here,

my homeland sits
in mourning for freedom.

I'm that captive,
and behind jail bars.
How can I breathe in
the air of freedom?

My wings broken,
I've fallen in the cage.
How can I fly
in the space of freedom?

When dying,
the soldier whispered:
"If only for a moment,
you would dress me
with the robe of freedom."

25

Every killer
was handed an ax in Kabul.
From every direction,
cries of grudge were raised in Kabul.

Did you see
when hair was shorn in Tehran?
When they set fire
on Farkhondeh in Kabul?

Tens of innocent girls
killed in Kaj School.
Coffins were handed
to fathers in Kabul.

They robbed us
of our destiny for good,
calling it
a divine decree in Kabul.

Everywhere innocents,
young and old, were killed.
Fake leader,
knuckleheads in Kabul.

They tossed our history
under their feet, crushing it.
They gave wings
to extremism in Kabul.

They bound our culture
with bolts and chains.
They inspired hostility
toward art in Kabul.

26

Banish rancor from your heart;
let us be kind.
Let us be of one pact,
one word, one tongue.

Let us bring a smile
to every child's lips.
Let us put a bit of bread
on every hungry person's table.

Among us, were someone
to set a fire of rage,
O Compatriot!
Let us put a fist to that mouth.

So long as the world exists,
evil shall not stop.
Lay your hand in mine
that we might be saved from it.

Our bow empty, yet
the enemy aims at us from all sides.
O Compatriot!
Let us be an arrow to the soul of the foe.

Stop stealing the cane
from the blind!
Let us be a parasol
to the poor people of ours.

In this heat,
for children
seeking shade,
let us be a patch of cloud in the sky.

I yearn for an embrace;
come open your arms to me.
Let us be of one body,
one spirit, and one soul.

27

The New Year came,
but my father didn't.
He never came back
to that ruined house.

They say father is gone,
never coming back.
Perhaps because
he bears no gifts to give.

I sat under the plum tree
for a moment at dusk.
Night fell, yet
father didn't come to the house.

Leyla's father bought her a dress
for the New Year;
yet my father didn't come
with even a cheap bracelet.

After my father,
no one ever told another story;
nor did any tale
come to my mother's memory.

28

The enemy has laid a trap
before my feet and yours.
They have choked in the throat
my voice and yours.

O Compatriot,
since you asked help
from the foreigner,
it has turned dark,
my air and yours.

From the moment
you and I were divided,
cold and numbing
has become my space and yours.

When we bashed the face
and head of the others,
they piled on the lamenting
and my mourning and yours.

Gift a rose,
not rockets and bombs.
All will be amazed
at my way and yours.

Until we embrace
and become brothers,
never shall be granted,
my prayers and yours.

We are one body and one soul,
you and I, my dear.
May the head of the enemy
be severed by my pain and yours.

Our town, home, and roof,
our door all shared.
Until you come to your senses,
this is my penance and yours.

29

In my hand, the flag,
on my lips, the chant of freedom.
Marching toward victory,
walking toward freedom.

To protect the homeland,
decisively you fight,
that I can breathe
the air of freedom.

My wings, broken,
I am thrown in a cage.
Come that I fly
in the space of freedom.

See that I am lost
amidst fire and smoke.
Raise the banner
for the sake of freedom.

You are my hope
and the desire of thirsty lips.
Only you remain
to fight for freedom.

Come, the cloth of captivity
is tormenting me.
Come, dress me only
in the robe of freedom.

30

Why are you lonely and tired,
O Homeland?
Why are you silent and broken,
O Homeland?

Why is your weather
always cold and stormy?

Why are you always
in mourning,
O Homeland?

Wherever the poplar
rises its head,
for every sharp ax,
you are its handle,
O Homeland!

For your gloomy state,
my eyes shed blood every night.
How severed, torn,
and disjointed you are,
O Homeland!

You hit your own foot
with an ax every moment.
You are tied up
with your own rope,
O Homeland!

31

How foolish, lowly,
and silly we have become.
How proud of worldly goods
and rank we have become.

We pounded
on each other's doors from spite.
How evil and wicked
we have become.

Though our nest rests
on the needle of a pine,
what happened that so distant
from this nest we have become?

They buried us
like chess pieces.

Into the depth of disaster
we went, and slain
we have become.

When we bowed
before the deceitful,
bit by bit, inch by inch,
searched we have become.

With every obstacle
and rope they bound us.
We died a thousand times,
and revived we have become.

We plotted
the suicide bombing
in our head.
Lost in the thought
of reaching the Houries
we have become.

32

When I'm tired,
speak not.
Of kisses, smiles,
and embraces,
speak not.

When my heart yearns
not for the rose
and the rose garden,
of lilacs, poppies,
and jasmines,
speak not.

With Joseph
who's been forgotten
by the caravan,
of the dread

of cliffs and plains,
speak not.

When you go
before Jacob,
of wolves, devouring,
and shirts,
speak not.

Do not test
my patience
and my resilience.
Of every widow's rancor,
sighs, and tears,
speak not.

When I am twisted
in pain,
of the misery and weariness
of my compatriots,
speak not.

With a broken-hearted,
mourning mother,
of suicide bombing
and maiming,
speak not.

With a wife
who's awaiting
good news,
of martyrdom, blood,
and shrouds,
speak not.

When the whole body
is moist from tears shed,
of clouds, thunder,
and rain,
speak not.

When my body
was prey to a bomb,
of flesh torn apart,
to the grave digger,
speak not.

33

We must change
the east wind route.
We must change
the village air.

Shouts are stifled
inside the throat.
We must change
the tune in the throats.

Nowhere will we get
with dormant cries.
We must change
the voice from its roots.

Medicine heals
our wounds no more.
Let us think together;
we must change the cure.

The film's scenario should go
in a different way.
If needed,
we must change
the camera shots.

Here in the town,
the weather is cold.
From now on,
we must change
the route of lightning strikes.

With this walking cane,
we will not reach our destiny.
With our own hands,
we must change the cane.

Put your hand in mine,
open your embrace to me,
that we might become a fist;
we must change this catastrophe.

34

I always wished
to be your walking cane,
but I failed.
For a moment,
to be the dust under your feet,
but I failed.

Mother,
I could never repay
my debt to you.
I always wished
to be the cure to all your pains,
but I failed.

Mother,
forgive me,
for in the ship of life,
I always wished
to always be your captain,
but I failed.

In the shadow
of your love and kindness,
I always wished
to be your attentive child,
but I failed.

I know
I have no place
in paradise.
If only I could follow
in your footsteps,
but I failed.

Mother,
forgive me
your white pure milk.
If only I could be
your loyal child, but I failed.

O Mother!
Your only hope
and wish was this:
For me to be a mirror
reflecting you,
but I failed.

Next to your bent stature,
you wished that
I always stand tall,
but I failed.

Life's mortar
pounded hard
on my head.
I'd be singing
in harmony with you,
but I failed.

Mother,
forgive me
that in this life,
for a moment
I'd be sacrificed for you,
but I failed.

Mother,
look how powerless
I've become.
I'd breathe
the same air as you,
but I failed.

Mother,
Come give me
another chance;
I wished
to be your walking cane,
but I failed.

35

Where is the one
to give a cane
to those who can walk no more?
To take a message of compassion
to the destitute generation?

Where is the one
to take by every branch
of a tall pine
the melodious air
to the fine-singing birds?

To the fallen soldier
who can walk no more,
who is there
to take a balm
to his fresh wound?

I sat
in the middle of the road,
hoping that
a damned friend
would take me

to the road's edge,
to be left alone.

I've fallen
in the middle of the road,
unable to walk.
If only someone
would come
to take us to its end.

Like a boat
lost in stormy water,
if only the sound
of a cry
would take us to a captain.

I'm in the middle of the road,
awaiting an incident
to scatter my body parts
in every direction.

36

Here, if you raise your head,
you'll be killed.
Even if you wear armor,
you'll be killed.

You must act
according to the script
you've been given.
If you follow another plan,
you'll be killed.

They've turned the gate
into a wall
in front of your face.
If you pull open
a door one day,
you'll be killed.

Like a pigeon
caught in a cage,
if you open your wings
to fly,
you'll be killed.

You must enter
the idol-filled temple.
Yet, if you draw an ax
from your belt,
you'll be killed.

Here, the voice
has been caught
in the throat.
If you tell tales
for a moment,
you'll be killed.

37

Ghazni, Balkh, Badakhshan,
Sar-e Pol, bloody;
Faryab, Kunar, Logar,
Kabul, bloody.

The homeland's sky
covered in black clouds;
the body of Zabul
lying motionless, bloody.

The stage, empty;
the air, smoky;
the space, polluted.
The bodies
of the homeland's soldiers,
the patrols, bloody.

It's blood that has filled
the tulips' chest.

Marigolds, jasmines, lilies,
hyacinths, bloody.

The garden, wounded;
the earth, tired;
the flower, withered.
Branches, leaves,
and body
of every rose bush, bloody.

My compatriots' blood
flowing in the street;
face and hair,
all disheveled, bloody.

38

O evil times!
O era of madness!
O century of horror and cruelty!
O age of collapse!

O absolute,
despotic commander
of the time!
Stop this senseless deception
and trickery!

We have been set ablaze
by your arrogance and pride.
Add no more
to our sorrow and pain.

O Mother
of the homeland!
To make it all end,
breathe out from your chest
a sigh full of sorrow.

We are thirsty people
drowned in blood,

We are being killed
by these statesmen.

O broken-winged bird!
Take my regards
to the valley of violence
and the land of blood.

39

What of the broken heart
and the destroyed spirit?
What of promises, pacts,
and pledges?

You made a promise,
yet you broke it.
What of the discussion
of God and respect
for the Koran?

Now that our heart's meadows
have withered,
what of the spring cloud
and the rain drop?

You sat at my table,
and we became brothers.
Now what of regard
for bread and butter?

You came to our home
by your own will.
What of the story
of the shepherd and the lost sheep?

All our life,
we've followed you
in uncertainty.

What of this hidden work
behind the veil?

You're breaking
all promises.
What of me
regretting my pledge?

So what
if we're friends no more?
What of fists, fights,
and wars?

40

In our city,
the mad and the sane
both laugh.
At home
and in the market,
they laugh.

Drowned in their own world,
the mad laugh.
Though, why are the sane
laughing so?

A city
on every corner of which,
lies the corpse
of a murder victim.
The whole world
is laughing
at our sick land.

A city
where,
in any hundred meters,
there's not one safe spot.

The government laughs
at the news headlines.

At the place
where I've been teaching
for a lifetime,
professors laugh
at the condition
of lecturers.

Everywhere,
in every corner,
in the street
and on the road,
everyone laughs
at his own condition.

Here, no one knows
the reason for laughter.
The official laughs
at the director's words
out of obligation.

At times asleep;
at times awake;
at times sober;
at times drunk.
On and on,
and on and on,
they laugh.

41

Look how we lost our head,
our feet, and our body,
how we became displaced,
homeless, and nationless.

Whoever came
with a marching band,

we stood,
clicking our heels.
Heedless,
we sank
into the sludge.

Whoever we befriended
became snakes
in the grass to us.
Still alive,
we were wrapped
in our shroud.

We lost
the gamble of life
this way.
We became shirtless,
naked, and penniless.

Perhaps in this exchange,
we are to blame.
With a flood of tears,
we set off into the desert
and the barren plains.

I don't care
what we were
and how we changed.
We became thieves,
lewd, and owners
of property and wives.

42

They have robbed the sun
from the sky of my nation.
They have robbed sleep
every night
from my mother's eyes.

I'm a flightless bird
who's lost the way
to my nest.
From atop the pines,
they have robbed me
of my feathers and wings.

Amidst these ruins,
I'm not at ease
for even a moment,
as they have robbed
the gown
from my soul.

What can I say?
Who can I tell?
Where can I begin?
In daylight
they have robbed my child
from our doorstep.

Head hidden
between her knees,
she is deep in thought.
They have robbed
my sister's smile
from her lips.

Whose shoulders
can I believe in now?
They have robbed me
of my trust,
my faith, and my support.

With whom can I share
the tale of my lonesomeness?
Now that they have robbed me
of my companion, my confidant,
and my comrade-in-arms.

43

Every moment,
criticism after criticism;
talk to me of solutions.
Talk to me of an answer
in a simple, ordinary way.

Of what use are plans,
theories, and agendas?
Step into the field
and talk for a moment about action.

Tell me not
of the cold months of winter.
Tell me of fresh days
and the first month of spring.

Do not add fuel
to the flames
of discrimination and difference.
Tell me a way
other than fire, war,
and debate.

For a long time,
I've been tasting
deadly poison.
Tell me of sugar, sweets,
and the taste of honey.

From the peak of imagination,
for my sake,
on one condition,
come sit next to me
and recite for me
a love poem.

Tell me of happy times,
of youth, and of bloom.
Tell me of myths,
of tales, and of proverbs.

44

It's hard to stay true
to one's colors
in this society;
to stay in tune
with this maimed society.

It's hard to be
in our society, so lost,
to stay without power
and without grace and glory.

Perhaps, our wavering
is the reason why
in this city,
we stay immersed
in chaos, riot,
and war.

A stone that is colored
on the outside only;
it's hard for us
to stay in the heart
of that stone.

Every moment here,
it's only the color
that's changed.
That's why
we have remained
without respect
and without shame.

45

In memory of the great poet Qahar Asi

Asi!
Look how your blood

is ignored!
How stones
have been thrown
on your grave.

Asi,
the wound of your existence
is still fresh, yet
the case of your slaying
is covered up.

Look how evil
is returning again;
How your murderers
are pardoned still.

Asi!
You're not here
to see the situation,
how convoluted
are the conditions
of this era.

Deals are made
with your blood.
The hands
of your murderers
are kissed.

The dealers
who sold your blood,
from their faces
all is discerned.

Asi!
In this business,
you are not alone.
The blood of thousands
like you
is being devoured.

46

I, and this destroyed mind
and strange feeling;
I, and this cursed life
and horrifying suffering.

Sorrow, pain, distress,
and this loneliness;
I, the displaced,
the distraught,
and this strange world.

Everyone sick, shriveled,
and fallen on the ground.
And in this city full of pain,
there is no healer.

O Heart!
What is this desire and excuse
and plea of yours?
Don't you have a share
in the joys
of the world?

Your destiny is set
like a piece of ice.
For in your next few steps,
death is waiting
close by.

47

Like autumn time,
I'm weary.
Autumn is tired of me,
and I, too, am weary.

The current unkindness
has made my heart sad.

Of them, of myself,
and of everything,
I'm weary.

My patience
has reached its end.
Of philosophical tales,
I'm weary.

The harpist Nakisa
and the poet Marvazi
have been silenced.
Of the story
of King Khosrow Parviz,
I'm weary.

Of Shirin's love
for Khosrow
and Khosrow's love
for her,
and of the hot breath
and neighing
of Khosrow's black stallion,
I'm weary.

Head to toe,
my being is enmeshed
in sorrow.
One after another,
continually,
bit by bit,
I'm weary.

Tonight,
I can't sleep
for the fervor and cheering.
Of the morning bird's moaning,
I'm weary.

48

I've brought a bag
full of life stories and memories.
I've brought
a basket of smiles
from the city of Herat.

And from Jalal-Abad,
the scent of orange blossoms,
and water of life
from Kandahar
just for you.

Raisins from Ghazni
and mulberries from Panjshir
as souvenirs for you,
I've brought
a bit of sugar crystal
from Rumi's hometown.

Of Siyamoy and Jallali,
of King Zahhak
and the woman poet Rabia,
I've brought the story
of the Shamameh Buddha
with all their details.

Without a doubt,
the brothers
have thrown us in a well.
I've brought
the ladder of love
as a savior.

I've got stories
from every corner
of this land.
I've brought the scent of love
from all sides of the border.

O Compatriot,
put your hand on mine.
I've brought a solution
for peace and stability.

Stop crying,
O Compatriot!
I've brought you a souvenir.
I've brought laughter
to ward off the problems.

49

How dependent, distressed,
and despicable
we've become.
No sin committed, yet
daily drowned in blood
we've become.

To reach the ascension
of compassion,
how diminutive, disregarded,
and degraded
we've become.

As if
our nest lies
on a pine needle.
What befell us
that on this route
we've become?

Out of revenge,
we knocked down
our own doors.
Like a roofless
and pillarless house
we've become.

With good fortune,
we would have stayed
on this road and path.
Why?
What befell us
that this ill-fortuned
we've become?

50

Let my festering wound heal.
You've ruined my home;
may your home be ruined!

You who burnt my garden and home,
may your home be ruined,
How can one be so unconscionable?

Like Balkh and Andarab,
my eye is dripping blood.
Don't let Panjshir
turn into a graveyard.

I'm the Bakvah desert;
look at how dried out I've become.
Let there be water
that tulips may grow,
hyacinths and basils too.

Neither does he bestow happiness,
nor is he content.
May the days
of Satan's evil ways
come to an end.

My home is freezing cold,
my condition is winter.
Day after day,
I'm waiting
for summer to arrive.

O Heavens!
Please bring some rain.
I'm burning.
Be cloudy!
Let a bit of rain fall here.

51

From behind
the world's mountain peaks,
arise.
With a clear idea
and a great plan,
arise.

In the depth of the sky,
tear down the dark cloud.
Like the confidence of a pilot,
arise.

The wolves are ambushed
and howl and howl.
Like the pride of a shepherd,
arise.

Break the steel,
seek a way.
Like a flowing river,
arise.

Shake the world
with a loud roar.
With strength, pride,
and power,
arise.

They've blocked the path
in front and behind.
So, find a way;
from the middle,
arise.

No crime
have you committed;
then why be killed?
To guard your life
and your soul,
arise.

The cure to this pain
is only in fighting back.
To tackle this cancer,
arise.

52

They broke the branch,
they burnt the garden and the nest.
At night,
they killed the candle,
they burnt the moth.

They robbed us
of our history, our culture.
They burnt our stories,
tales, and myths.

They rolled up their sleeves
to be rid of us.
They burnt offices, courts,
palaces, and homes.

They tied
our hands, our feet
by foreign decree.
For which crime
have they set this home
on fire?

No one survived
their cruelty and tyranny.
They burnt the desire

of the crazed lover.

Our leaders
put on women's clothes
one by one.
They burnt
solemn male trust
and faith.

On whose shoulders
can I count now?
They put a sword
to the throat;
they burnt the shoulders.

This is not Kabul's pain;
it's all Persians' pain.
They burnt it all,
from Herat, Afghanistan,
to Fergana, Uzbekistan.

53

You fell,
and I asked
what happened?
Are you hurt?
No!
Don't you hate this ill fortune?
No!

You pursued
studies and school
your whole life.
So what?
Did you find a job?
No!

Every moment
you're wrestling

with rhymes.
So, do you have
a collection of poems?
No!

You winked an eye
and reflected light
from a mirror.
Did you fall in love
with the neighbor girl?
No!

The insane
are beautiful
with their craziness.
Did you become sane
by talking to the wise?
No!

You saw
every corner
of the world.
Did you learn
of the incident?
No!

Fate came
and whispered
in my ear:
"Did you wake up
from a heavy sleep
one night?"
No!

Fate keeps
asking me
every moment:
"You fell and rose.
Are you hurt?"
No!

54

We must leave
this city
right away.
We must go
to another city
or town.

Abraham's father
hasn't stopped
making idols.
We must rise quickly
and think only
of an ax.

Day and night
are pitch-black
for us.
This night of mourning
must soon become dawn.

People are awaiting
the whip every moment.
We must beware
of this city's ruler.

O Heart!
This city full of pain
is your place no more.
How long
must you be clothed
in sorrow?

O Fellow Traveler!
Forget the tale
of this disaster.
We must begin talking
about this exodus.

55

Bury me
within the extent
of these borders.
Bury me
like the dark custom
of these times.

Wash my dead body
in Herat and Ghazni rivers.
In the earth of my homeland,
bury me with no excuse.

In the outskirts
of Pamir and Balkh,
and in the Hindu Kush,
in the earth
of my homeland,
bury me lovingly.

Do not weep
at the time of my death.
Bury me
with the music of lyrics,
poetically.

Bury me
under the mulberry trees
of my village,
in the shadow
of the wall
of my house.

For your prayer
to reach me,
bury me
in the beautiful village
of Astaneh.

Entrust me
to the outskirts

of this weary land.
With no tears,
just bury me secretly.

For the tired travelers
not to see my corpse,
bury me
in the earth
toward nighttime.

On my gravestone
write in tears:
"Stranger and Nationless."
Bury me humbly.

56

One window open,
another one closed.
One heart full of love,
another one broken.

At times,
the opening dark,
at times, lit.
At times,
with a tranquil heart,
at times,
with a weary one.

For a lifetime
on a dark, scary road,
at times,
we are standing
in line,
at times in groups.

On a broken boat,
we are flowing

on every wave,
at times, alone,
at times, in crowds.

I've knocked
on heart's door,
O Love!
Where are you?
They said
you are sitting
in mourning for fate.

57

The flower
had blossoms, yet
spring was bare.
And everywhere,
the garden was bare
of plane trees.

Everywhere trees
were green
and full of fruit.
The apple tree
was sick,
the pomegranate tree bare.

The sky
of the village,
moonlit as always.
By the window,
at nighttime,
the beloved was not there.

On their shoulders,
each had a clay pot,
searching for water.
Among all those beauties,
my beloved's place was bare.

All were going
toward the village
in a line.
Lips thirsty, yet
the river was bare.

The air of the village
gave me no peace.
It had worth
or value no more.

They killed swiftly
the village tree
with an ax.
Its shadow, though,
was awaiting no one.

The travelers
all returned midway.
Long journey, yet
their bags were bare.

I was a traveler
who saw
strangers everywhere,
sitting by myself
with no one by my side.

58

Once again,
blood and condemnation;
once again,
the same old words.
Once again,
tears, moans, and regret;
once again,
sighing, crying, and wailing.

Once again,
a mother mourning
for her son;
once again,
a sister sitting
by the grave.
O Mother!
Condolences!
Once again,
patience, and again,
sympathy.

Once again,
on the wall,
a remnant
of her son's red blood.
Once again,
she is sitting
in mourning,
again in sorrow
and bereavement.

Once again,
ambulance sirens
from every side;
once again,
behind the hospital door.
Once again,
carrying out the coffin;
once again,
those difficult moments.

Once again,
corpses and burials
on every side;
once again,
unidentified victims.
Once again,
the red blood

of thousands of my people
flowing on the roads.

59

Mother!
Look how they've torn
my body.
How these hyenas
have torn
my clothes.

Mother!
Come look
at your son's state.
They've torn me
from limb
to limb.

Jacob unaware
of his Joseph's state.
The wolves of Egypt
have torn
my shirt.

Mother!
Come to me
with needle and thread.
Sew swiftly,
for they've torn
my shroud.

No chance for me
to die in comfort
and peace,
for they've even torn
my struggling feet and hands.

At night
when my child asks

about my absence,
tell him
that they've torn
my body.

Mother!
I didn't burn
in the tumult alone.
I feel
with my whole being
that they've torn
my homeland.

60

I've gotten used to
ill and sad nights.
I've gotten used to
this restless condition.

The cup
of my patience
and hope
is brimming over.
I've gotten used to
expectation and waiting.

I hear
no crying here.
I've gotten used to
the thief's cruelty.

Everywhere I hear moaning,
shouting, mourning.
I've gotten used to
gunpowder and explosions.

I fear not wounds
and thorny desert bushes.

I've gotten used to
the pain of thorns.

My fortune dark,
my fate destroyed.
I've gotten used to
this feeling
and this life.

I've tasted so much
of the enemy's bitter poison,
that I've gotten used to
snakes' venom.

61

I desire
a free disposition
for myself.
Take me
to Khorasan.
Take me
to Isfahan, Ghor,
Yazd, and Tajikistan.

Mashhad and Pamir,
Balkh and Sughd,
and Kabul, my home.
Marv is calling me;
take me to Samangan.

My being, my soul,
my body and life,
all Persian.
To revive me,
take me
to Kulob and Tehran.

Khayyam, Jami,
and Biruni,

my ancestors.
Take me
to the shrine
of Nasir Khusraw
in Badakhshan.

We have
the same tongue,
the same race,
the same faith.
Take me
to Tus,
Vakhsh, Farkhar,
and Shebreghan.

O Samarkand!
O Bukhara!
O my whole being!
Have compassion
and take me
to Khatlon.

How can London,
Paris, and Moscow
compete with Herat?
Take me
to the Panjshir valley,
Varzob, and Khuzestan.

My patience
is wearing thin
from being alone
in this country.
Take me
to Gholghondi,
Salang, and Paghman.

I ask
of my friends
that after my death,
they take me

for burial
to my birthplace, Keraman.

62

My nature, my love,
my whole being, Persian.
My existence, my soul,
my warp and weft are Persian.

My prayer rug, Balkh;
my prayer beads and mantra,
Rumi's Masnavi.
My Imam, Hafez and Jami;
my greeting is Persian.

My school, Iqbal and Bedil;
my lesson, Ferdowsi.
My pillar of support, Saʿdi;
my being is Persian.

My birthplace, Marv;
my home, Tehran
and Dushanbe.
My accent, pearl of Dari;
my speech is Persian.

My guide, Avicenna;
my history, *Shahnameh*.
My tone, voice, melody,
and poems are Persian

Jami's Haft-Awrang, my pride;
Ganjavi, my honor.
My moon and sun,
my morning and night,
my every hour is Persian.

Hear Rudaki's poem
from the lamenting reed flute.

My tar, tanbur,
and rubab,
my lute and harp,
are all Persian.

63

I'll get used to
the stupid and the smart,
in the end.
I'll get used to
the streets and the markets,
in the end.

If I stay
in this city
a single day more,
I'll get used to
the drugs and the cigarettes,
in the end.

I'll get used to
the poor sister,
the confusion,
and the sick mother,
in the end.

I detest fire
and guns, yet
I'll get used to
the archer,
in the end.

I figure
from the state
of the homeland today,
That I'll get used to
the kohl and turbans,
in the end.

I'm amazed
at this soulless regime, yet
I'll get used to
these secrecies and mysteries,
in the end.

Though I've been raised
in fire and smoke,
I'll get used to
the mourning city,
in the end.

I intend to forsake
this sorrowful city,
I'll get used to
the strangers,
in the end.

I'll leave the country
to stay alive.
Bit by bit,
I'll get used to everything,
in the end.

I'm the detested,
oppressed generation
of this time.
I'll get used to
this pitiful status,
in the end.

I am the Sufi Hallaj,
and I reveal secrets.
And I'll get used to
the gallows,
in the end.

۱

من کی‌ام؟ خود بیش‌تر از دیگران می‌دانی‌ام
از بدخشان و هراتم، تبعه‌ی ختلانی‌ام

آذرخش روشنم در آسمان تیرگی
زاده‌ی بلخ و بخارایم، یلِ سامانی‌ام

من که پور رستم و سهرابم و از کی‌قباد
از نژاد و گوهر و از نطفه‌ی ساسانی‌ام

درس آزادی بدادم اردشیر بابکان
از گروه خسرو ام از ریشه‌ی شاهانی‌ام

از پدر میراث دارم غیرت و مردانگی
کس که نتوانست مغلوبم، تو هم نتوانی‌ام

نغمه‌های باربد قلبم نوازش داده است
من ز نسل آریا، از نوه‌ی سلطانی‌ام

رهرو اندیشه‌ی سامان و از بومسلم‌ام
ناجیِ هرلحظه و هر دوره‌ی طوفانی‌ام

خوب می‌دانی تو از فرهنگ و از تاریخ ما
من برای دیگران آیینه‌ی انسانی‌ام

تاجِکم من، تاجِکم، آری اصیلاً تاجِکم
از تو من ترسی ندارم، از چه می‌ترسانی‌ام؟

۲

دیدی چه سهل و ساده وطن را فروختند
این خانه‌ی قدیم و کهن را فروختند

بستند تا ابد دهنِ اعتراض را
از لب تمام حرف و سخن را فروختند

سخت است باورش، چه بگویم برای‌تان؟
از گور هر شهید، کفن را فروختند

هرجا درون خانه ی هر اجنبی شدند
این گونه روسپی شده تن را فروختند

نفرین به این معامله و فکر خام شان
حتی که عضو عضو بدن را فروختند

حالا چه پشت سرحد و مرزش گرفته اند
وقتی که کوه و دشت و دمن را فروختند

۳

باور مکن به قامت و براستواری‌ام
من جسم زخم خورده‌ی یک انتحاری‌ام

مانند زخم‌های تَرَک خورده در بدن ـ
خونابه‌ام که از تنِ بیمار جاری‌ام

عمری‌ست در میان قفس گیر کرده‌ام
من بال و پر شکسته‌ی مرغ قناری‌ام

ما را ز شهر و دهکده تبعید کرده‌اند
دیری‌ست من ز شهر شماها فراری‌ام

بُغضم که در میان گلو گیر کرده‌ام
روزی رسد که تا ز گلوگاه براری‌ام

دیگر مرا به حال خودِ من رها کنید
من درد لاعلاجم و بیمارِ ساری‌ام

عادت به فصل و موسم پاییز کرده‌ام
گل‌های ناشکفته‌ی فصل بهاری‌ام

دیگر توان و صبر مرا امتحان مکن
من جسم زخم خورده‌ی یک انتحاری‌ام!

۴

دگر به کوفه مرو، دشت کربلا این‌جاست
تمام واقعه و مرگ و ماجرا این‌جاست

ببین که میهنِ من غرق و خفته در خون است
به هرسو می‌نگرم شیون و عزا این‌جاست

چه‌گونه دردِ و غمم را به دل نگه دارم
غمی که می‌کشدم سوی قهقرا این‌جاست

بیا و حادثه‌ی کربلا دوباره ببین
حسین بی‌سر و بی‌جان و دست و پا، این‌جاست

دگر به کشتیِ ویرانه بر نمی‌گردم
سری بریده‌َ و بی‌جان ناخدا این‌جاست

چه‌گونه، با چه امیدی به خانه دل بندم
هزار فتنه و صد کفر و ناروا این‌جاست

دگر از این وطنم خواهش و امیدی نیست
کسی که رفته فقط سوی انزوا، این‌جاست

۵

دفترچه‌ام که در دل هر باد رفته‌ام
صیدم که خود به دامن صیاد رفته‌ام

یعقوب را خبر برسانید، ساربان!
من یوسفِ ز قافله از یاد رفته‌ام

شهری به مثل کابلِ در خون تپیده‌ای
در ظلم و در جهالَت و بیداد رفته‌ام

هر برج و گوشه‌ام به دل خاک خفته است
دیواره‌ای ز ریشه و بنیاد رفته‌ام

جرمی نکرده‌ام که بَرندم به پای دار
با پای خود به خانه‌ی جلاد رفته‌ام

پوسیده‌ام، ورق زده و پاره ـ پاره‌ام
هرسو مرا که باد فرستاد، رفته‌ام!

۶

تا مساعد گشت فُرصت‌ها، زمان از دست رفت
سفره‌ی امید خالی گشت، نان از دست رفت

فصل عشق آخر رسید و موسم پاییز شد
بادهای تند سر شد، آشیان از دست رفت

یوسفِ گم گشته‌ام، افتاده‌ام در بین چاه
بهر بیرون کردن من کاروان از دست رفت

تکیه‌گاهم روزها در سایه‌ی دیوار بود
واژگون دیوارها شد، سایه‌بان از دست رفت

دست خالی پس چه‌خواهم کرد با کفتارها
تیرهاَ یک ـ یک خطا شد تا کمان از دست رفت

۷

خونِ دل خود جای غذا تجربه کردیم
ما گریه جدا، درد جدا تجربه کردیم

ما نسل ستم‌دیده و مظلوم زمانیم
دردی همه را حیف که ما تجربه کردیم

جز درد و غم غصه و جز آتش و وحشت
ما شادی و لب‌خند کجا تجربه کردیم؟

فریاد و صدا را به گلوها خفه کردیم
ما اسلحه را شکل عصا تجربه کردیم

بیرون شده از کوره و سر سخت‌ترینیم
هر حادثه را حین بلا تجربه کردیم

کشتیم و شکستیم و ببستیم، در آخر ـ
خونِ همه را مثل حنا تجربه کردیم

ما درد کشیدیم و صدایی نکشیدیم
صبر دل خود جای دوا تجربه کردیم

در صفحه‌ی تاریخ چنین وضع ندیدیم
تحلیف دو شه را به خدا تجربه کردیم

۸

من پورِ بلخ و سُغد و سمنگانی‌ام هنوز
رزم‌آورِ شجاع خراسانی‌ام هنوز

جاری‌ست خون خسروِ پرویز در رگم
حماسه‌ساز دوره‌ی ساسانی‌ام هنوز

رستم نمرده، آرش و سهراب زنده‌اند
اسطوره‌های عصر درخشانی‌ام هنوز

هرجا درفش کاوه بلند است، او منم
من پهلوان دوره‌ی شاهانی‌ام هنوز

جسمم ز کابل است و بخارا روان من
من از سپاه دوره‌ی سامانی‌ام هنوز

هرچند زخم‌های تنم تازه است و لیک ـ
لب‌خند لحظه‌های پریشانی‌ام هنوز

ز بادهای ساده نلرزیده قامتم
ناجیِ درد دوره‌ی طوفانی‌ام هنوز

تا قهرمان قصه ابومسلم است و من ـ
نه مُرده‌ام، نه قصه‌ی پایانی‌ام هنوز

بام جهان قلمرو حاکمیت من است
من مرد با غرور بدخشانی‌ام هنوز

مرزی اگر کشیده زمان بین‌مان؛ ولی ـ
من از خُجند و مشهد و ختلانی‌ام هنوز

من از هرات و تو ز بخارا و اصفهان
می‌دانمت، مگر تو نمی‌دانی‌ام هنوز

هرچند از چنین همه اوصاف کوچکم
فرزند با وقار کرامانی‌ام هنوز

۹

ظاهراً خوبم؛ ولی روح و روانم خوب نیست
جسم من سر تا به پا تب کرده، جانم خوب نیست

قدرت حرف و سخن گفتن ندارم، بعد از این
خورده تا بر صورتم مشتی، دهانم خوب نیست

بر نشاط و چهره‌ی پر خنده‌ام هرگز مبین
باورم کن، بند ـ بندِ استخوانم خوب نیست

بعد از این میل غزل گفتن ندارم بر سرم
چند روزی می‌شود طبع روانم خوب نیست

لانه ام را بادهای تند ویران کرده است
بعد از این حال و هوای آشیانم خوب نیست

۱۰

زشت است، دگر جامه‌ی تن را نفروشید
هر قسمت و اجزای بدن را نفروشید

سودای تن هرچند به من ربط ندارد
پُردرد و حزین است، وطن را نفروشید

این خاک پر از خون شهید است خبردار!
از مُرده‌ی هر گور، کفن را نفروشید

این خاک اگر جایگهِ مادرتان هست
زین بیش دگر دشتَ و دمن را نفروشید

از خاک وطن سرمه بسازید و بمالید
گل سر زده در باغ، چمن را نفروشید

از تار محبت همه‌جا رشته ببافید
زنجیر بسازید و رسن را نفروشید

گر رشته‌ی این داد و ستُد را نبریدید
خود را بفروشید، و من را نفروشید!

۱۱

مثل یک خانه‌ی ویرانه فرو ریخته‌ام
از سر و قامت و از شانه فرو ریخته‌ام

چند روزی‌ست که با سنگ به بالم زده‌اند
مثل یک فاخته، از لانه فرو ریخته‌ام

هرکه می‌بیند و برحالت من می‌خندد
مثل یک آدم دیوانه فرو ریخته‌ام

گرچه بر کنج دلی دوست ندارم جایی
تا که از دیده‌ی بیگانه فرو ریخته‌ام

گل خُشکی که به دیوار نمی‌چسپم من
از در و دَور و برِ خانه فرو ریخته‌ام

۱۲

با چه موجودات بی‌فرهنگ گیر افتاده‌ایم
در عذاب خصم و رفتار شریر افتاده‌ایم

غیر انسانی بود سیمای نامیمون‌شان
زیر چنگ کرکس و کفتار پیر افتاده‌ایم

شمّه‌ای از آدمیت نیست در افکارشان
ما به چنگال غلامان اجیر افتاده‌ایم

جز قلم دیگر سلاحی نیست اندر دست ما
با چه‌حال و روز و با شکل حقیر افتاده‌ایم

شاخه بشکستند باغ و خانه را آتش زدند
در دیار تشنه و دشت کویر افتاده‌ایم

کینه‌توزی‌های‌شان روزی به پایان می‌رسد
هرچه می‌خواهند، حالا ما که خیر افتاده‌ایم

روز قصد و انتقام آخر فرا خواهد رسید
حال در چنگ شغالان، ناگزیر افتاده‌ایم

۱۳

کی شود پُنبه و تابوت سفارش‌ندهیم؟
پی هر حادثه باروت سفارش ندهیم

پای هم‌میهن من قطع نگردد دیگر
پای مصنوعیِ او بوت سفارش ندهیم

بهر هر شاخه‌ی پرمیوه و هر ساقه‌ی سبز
تیشه از عالم لاهوت سفارش ندهیم

یوسف از سوی برادر نرود در تهِ چاه
کی شود چاله و برهوت سفارش ندهیم

پی یک لقمه غذا هرسو نباشیم روان
روی هر جاده دگر قوت سفارش ندهیم

جنگ برچیده شود، صلح بیاید این‌جا
کی شود پنبه و تابوت سفارش ندهیم؟

۱۴

سوداگران چه‌ساده تن و جان فروختند
شأن و غرور و عزت و وجدان فروختند

بهر مقام و شوکت و جا و جلال خویش
دردا که هست و بودِ خود آسان فروختند

حقی که خون‌بهای هزاران شهیدِ ما
این ناکسان چه‌ساده و ارزان فروختند

ایشان جز از معامله کاری نکرده‌اند
بهر بقا و بودِ خود، ایمان فروختند

ما خود هنوز زنده، حق و امتیاز ما ـ
سرّیِ و مخفیانه و پنهان فروختند

حتی که پاسِ آب و نمک را نکرده‌اند
خوردند آبَ و نان، نمک‌دان فروختند

خودکرده را نه درد و نه درمان بود؛ ولی
افسوس و صد دریغ، که انسان فروختند

دردم نمی‌کند به فروش سر و تنش
دردا که نام نیک خراسان فروختند!

۱۵

در هوای صاف، باران را تحمل می‌کنیم
ظلم استبداد دوران را تحمل می‌کنیم

تا توقف می‌دهد ابلیس طرحِ جنگ را
بی‌محابا کار شیطان را تحمل می‌کنیم

تا نیاید پرچم آزادگی در اهتزاز
شش‌پَر و زنجیرِ زندان را تحمل می‌کنیم

تا که از روی حقیقت پرده برداری شود ـ
چند روزی راز پنهان را تحمل می‌کنیم

تا نیاید موسم نیلوفر و مریم، فقط ـ
سردی و برف زمستان را تحمل می‌کنیم

می‌نشینیم این‌که وضع مملکت بهتر شود
حالت و اوضاع بحران را تحمل می‌کنیم

تا که خون می‌بارد از جغرافیای میهنم
ناله و دردِ خراسان را تحمل می‌کنیم

۱۶

چه عجب حالت غم‌انگیزی، چه عجب سخت امتحانی بود
نه به اشکم مجاَل آرامش، نه به بغضم دگر امانی بود

تا کهِ من جانبش نگه کردم، سوی من خنده‌ی ملیحی زد
نسبتاً رخت کهنه بر تن داشت، دختر تازه، نوجوانی بود

بسته‌ی ساجقی به دستش داشت، بود اِستاده پشت رستوران
از پسِ دربِ رستوران، چشم او سوی لقمه‌نانی بود

کوهی از درد روی شانه‌ی او، عالمی اشک بر دو چشمانش
درگلوی گرفته‌اش دیدم، غصه و بغض بی‌کرانی بود

تا که پرسیدم از گذشته‌ی او، یک‌به‌یک گفت داستانش را
نان و آبی برای‌مان می‌داد، پدرم مرد قهرمانی بود

همه در زیر سقف یک خانه، زندگی خوب و خوب‌تر می‌شد
تا که محتاج این و آن نشویم، او به مانند سایبانی بود

پدرم رفت و برنگشت آخر، طعمه‌ی موج انتحاری شد
هرچه غم بود، ریخت خانه‌ی ما، هرچه در روی آسمانی بود

اشک از لای مژه‌های سیاش، تاکه می‌ریخت روی سینه‌ی خاک
آه... آن لحظه‌ها چه عجب، یک تراژیدیِ گرانی بود

تا شنیدم حکایت او را، حال از حال من برفت، آخر
نه دگر قدرتی به پای من، نه برایم دگر بیانی بود

هرچه پولی به جیب‌هایم بود، ریختم روی دامنش، یک‌دم-
موجی از خنده در لبانی او، شبیه نور کهکشانی بود

یک به‌یک بغض و غصه‌هایم را، از درون دلم برون کردم
گریه کردم تمام آن ساعت، تا به من قدرت و توانی بود

بغض من در دم گلو ناگه، مثل خمپاره انفجار نمود
چه عجب حالت غم‌انگیزی، چه عجب سخت امتحانی بود

۱۷

این‌جا غرور و شأن و فـَرم را شکسته‌اند
دیوار و سقف و بام و درم را شکسته‌اند

مانند تک درخت سپیدار کنج باغ-
زرشاخه‌های دور و برم را شکسته‌اند

دستم بگیر و درس شهامت بده خلیل!
این قوم آزری، تبرم را شکسته اند

خواهم که زندگی بکنم با سرِ بلند
این‌گونه دست و پا و سرم را شکسته‌اند

می‌خواستم که پر بزنم در فضای عشق
اما ببین که بال و پرم را شکسته‌اند

۱۸

مادری بار دگر چشم به راهِ پسر است
پسری بار دگر خیره به راهِ پدر است

کودکی چشم به تصویر پدر دوخته است
خواهری بار دگر منتظر یک خبر است

گاه بر پنجره بسته‌ست دو چشمانش را
گاه هم خیره و سرگشته نگاهش به در است

قامتش در غم و اندوه پسر خم گشته
هردو دستان پدر بار دگر در کمر است

حلقه افتاده ز دستان دو دل‌داده، دگر
مثل یک تازه عروسی که مگر در سفر است

سفره‌ی قبر کنان پر ز غذاهای لذیذ
باز لب‌خند کفن‌دوز امیدِ ظفر است

باز خونین شده دیوار و درِ میهن من
مردمانش بِنگر بی‌تن و بی‌پا و سر است

۱۹

زندگی در هاله‌ی ابهام باقی مانده است
پای عمر ما فقط در دام باقی مانده است

در زبان و گفته‌های مردم این کشورم
حرف زشت و واژه‌ی دشنام باقی مانده است

بی‌گمان در سرزمینی زندگی دارم، فقط
بهرشان انسانیت در نام باقی مانده است

پختگی جایی ندارد در نگاه ما دگر
باور و اندیشه‌ی ما خام باقی مانده است

با صدای گریه هردم باز شد چشمان ما
طعم تلخ دشمنی در کام باقی مانده است

مُرده‌ام این‌جا، مگر روحم نمی‌دانم کجاست
جسم من در پایه‌ی اعدام باقی مانده است

۲۰

من که با پای پر از آبله، باید بروم
با شکیبایی و با حوصله، باید بروم

تا که در گرد و غبارِ وطنم گم نشوم
من به دنبال همین قافله باید بروم

گرچه بیداد زمان پای مرا بسته، مگر ـ
با همین قید و همین سلسله باید بروم

گر بخواهم نفسی راحت و آسوده کشم
از بلا و ستم نازله باید بروم

تا که من هیزم این آتش دوران نشوم
در همین وقت و همین فاصله، باید بروم

۲۱

دگر بهانه ندارم، دوباره برگردم
امید خانه ندارم، دوباره برگردم

هوای شعر تو کوچیده از سرم، دیری‌ست
دگر ترانه ندارم، دوباره برگردم

خیال و خاطر آسوده بعد رفتن خویش ـ
به آن کرانه ندارم، دوباره برگردم

رفیق همدم و از جان گذشته‌یی، دیگر
در این زمانه ندارم، دوباره برگردم

سری که از ته دل، صادقانه بگذارد
به‌روی شانه ندارم، دوباره برگردم

۲۲

برای من دعا کن، روز سختی پیش رو دارم
خدا را التجا کن، روز سختی پیش رو دارم

بلا این‌روزها از هرسو ما را در کمین دارد
بیا رفع بلا کن روز سختی پیش رو دارم

من از تو جز دعا چیزی نمی‌خواهم، عزیز من!
به حرفم اعتنا کن، روز سختی پیش رو دارم

دعای نیمه‌شب شاید قبول حق شود، با من
خودت را هم‌صدا کن، روز سختی پیش رو دارم

تو گفتی از دعا هرگز فراموشم نمی‌سازی
بیا دَینت ادا کن، روز سختی پیش رو دارم

به این بیگانه‌گی‌ها بیش‌تر بیگانه می‌گردی
خودت را آشنا کن، روز سختی پیش رو دارم

۲۳

برف و یخ و سرمای زمستان متفاوت
جرم و گنه و گوشه‌ی زندان متفاوت

گرگان به کمین‌اند و بیابان همه خاموش
کوه و کمر و هی - هی چوپان متفاوت

نه دشمن ما دشمن و نه دوست، دگر دوست
جنگ و جدل و دست و گریبان متفاوت

از حال بدِ مردم کندز چه بگویم
بلخ از همه ویرانه، بدخشان متفاوت

آسایش تخار به هم خورده در این روز
بنگی شده مخروبه، کلفگان متفاوت

خاموش شده نعره‌ی تکبیر شمالی
پریان به هم خورده و پروان متفاوت

سرد است دگر حال و هوای پلخمری
از جلگه چه گویم، همه بغلان متفاوت

از حال دلی مردم غزنی تو نیایی
غور و کنر و لوگر و لغمان متفاوت

زابل که دگر شهر پر از کینه و درد است
شاجوی و قلات، اتغر و میزان متفاوت

حیرت زده‌ی شهر پر از درد هراتم
ادرسکن مخروبه و گلران متفاوت

از خون تو رنگین شده دریای هریرود
سنگین شده پر غصه و گلران متفاوت

المار و قرمقُل شده یک شهر پر از غم
خروار جدا مانده و زدران متفاوت

از شهر سمنگان و سرِپل گله‌ای نیست
قرقین همه ویرانه، شبَرغان متفاوت

خون می‌چکد از دیده‌ی هر فرد جنوبی
ارگون و سروبی و متاخان متفاوت

از آتش و از دود تو کابل به که گویم!
روزت همه تاریک، شبستان متفاوت

آدم، همه گویند ز یک عضو وجوداند
این گفته دروغ آمده، انسان متفاوت!

پر درد و پر از غصه بود زادگه من
هرساعت و هرلحظه کرامان متفاوت

ای میهن بی‌چاره و در خون شده‌ی من!
درد تو به جانم زده، درمان متفاوت

۲۴

کجاست آن‌که برزمد برای آزادی
به دست پرچم و بر لب نوای آزادی

کجاست آن‌که گذارد فقط برای وطن
قدم به سوی ظفر، پابه‌پای آزادی

اسیر دشمنم این‌جا، فقط اسیر خودم
کجاست مرشد و آن رهگشای آزادی

صدا میان گلو گیر مانده در این‌جا
نشسته میهن من در عزای آزادی

من آن اسیرم و در پشت میله‌ی زندان
چه‌سان نفس بکشم در هوای آزادی

شکسته بال و پر من، فتاده در قفسم
چه‌گونه پر بزنم در فضای آزادی

به وقت مردنش، عسکر به زیر لب می‌گفت:
که لحظه‌ای به تنم کن قبای آزادی

۲۵

بر دست هر قاتل تبر دادند، در کابل
هرسو شعار کینه سر دادند، در کابل

موی کسی دیدی‌که قیچی خورد در تهران؟
فرخنده را وقتی‌که در دادند، در کابل

در کاج ده‌ها دختر مظلوم را کشتند
تابوت را دست پدر دادند، در کابل

بر سرنوشت ما همیشه دست یازیدند
این کار را حَکم قَدَر دادند در کابل

در هرطرف پیر و جوان را بی‌گنه کشتند
رهبر نما را مغز خر دادند، در کابل

تاریخ ما را زیر پا بردند، لِه کردند
افراطیت را بال و پر دادند در کابل

فرهنگ ما را با غل و زنجیرها بستند
انگیزه برضدِ هنر دادند، در کابل

۲۶

ز قلبت کینه بیرون کن، بیا تا مهربان باشیم
بیا یک عهد و یک پیمان و یک حرف و زبان باشیم

بیا تا بر لبی هر کودک خود خنده را آریم
بیا بر سفره‌ی بیچاره‌ای یک لقمه نان باشیم

میان ما اگر هرکس که خواهد کینه افروزد
بیا ای هموطن! مشتی برای آن دهان باشیم

جهان تا است کی ابلیس دست از کار بر دارد
بده دستت به دستم تا زدستش در امان باشیم

کمان خالی و دشمن هرطرف ما را هدف دارد
بیا ای هموطن! تیری به جان دشمنان باشیم

عصا دزدیدنت را بس کن از دستان نابینا
بیا بر مردم درمانده‌ی خود سایبان باشیم

در این گرما برای کودکانی سایه می‌خواهند
بیا یک توته‌ای ابری به روی آسمان باشیم

دلم آغوش می‌خواهد بیا بر من بغل وا کن
بیا تا یک تن و یک جسم و یک روح و روان باشیم

۲۷

عید آمد و امّا پدرم خانه نیامد
هرگز طرفِ خانه‌ی ویرانه نیامد

گویند پدر رفته دگر باز نیاید
شاید جهت دادن عیدانه نیامد

در سایه‌ی آلوچه نشستم به دمی شام
شب شد، پدرم جانب کاشانه نیامد

لیلا، پدرش کُرته‌ی عیدانه خریده
حتی پدرم همره‌ی «دسوانه» نیامد

بعد از پدرم، هیچ دگر قصّه نگفتند
در خاطره‌ی مادرم افسانه نیامد

۲۸

تله بگذاشته دشمن دم پای من و تو
در گلوها خفه کرده‌ستَ صدای من و تو

هم‌وطن! تا تو ز بیگانه مدد خواسته‌ایی
تیره گشته‌ست دگر حال و هوای من و تو

از همان لحظه که بین من و تو تفرقه شد
سرد و بی‌حال و خنک گشته فضای من و تو

تا که بر صورت و بر فرق دگر کوبیدیم
میله کردند در اندوه و عزای من و تو

عوض راکت و بم، شاخه گلی هدیه بکن
همه حیران شود، این‌گونه برای من و تو

تا در آغوش نگیریم و برادر نشویم
پس اجابت نشود ذکر و دعای من و تو

من و تو یک تن و یک روح و روانیم، عزیز!
سر دشمن بزند درد و بلای من و تو

قریه و خانه و بام و در ما مشترک است
تا نیایی به خود، این است سزای من و تو

۲۹

به دست، پرچم و بر لب نوای آزادی
قدم به سوی ظفر پا به پای آزادی

برای حفظ وطن قاطعانه می‌رزمی
که تا نفس بکشم در هوای آزادی

شکسته بال و پرِ من، فتاده در قفسم
بیا که پر بزنم در فضای آزادی

ببین که گُم شده‌ام در میان آتش و دود
به اهتزاز بیاور لوای آزادی

تویی امید من و آرزوی تشنه‌لبان
فقط تویی که برزمی برای آزادی

بیا لباس اسارت عذاب می‌دهدم
بیا فقط به تنم کن قبای آزادی

۳۰

چرا تو بی‌کس و تنها و خسته‌ای، میهن!
چرا تو ساکت و درهم شکسته‌ای، میهن!

چرا هوای تو همواره سرد و طوفانی‌ست
چرا همیشه به ماتم نشسته‌ای، میهن!

به هرکجا که سپیدار، تازه سر بکشد
برای هر تبری تیز، دسته‌ای، میهن!

به حال زار تو خون گریه می‌کنم هرشب
جدا و پاره و از هم مگو میهن!

تو خود به پای خودت تیشه می‌زنی هردم
تو با طناب خودت، سخت بسته‌ای، میهن!

۳۱

چه‌قدر بی‌خِرد و پست و بی‌شعور شدیم
به مال و هستیِ دنیا چه حد غرور شدیم

ز روی کینه به درهای خویش کوبیدیم
چه‌قدر آدم بدکاره و شرور شدیم

اگرچه لانه‌ی‌مان روی برگ یک کاج است
مگر چه شد؟ که از این آشیانه دور شدیم

مثال مهره‌ی شطرنج، چال‌مان دادند
به عمق فاجعه رفتیم و تا ترور شدیم

به پای مردم مکاره تا که خم گشتیم
و ذره ـ ذره، وجب بر وجب مرور شدیم

به هر موانع و بندی که گیرمان دادند
هزار مرتبه مُردیم و نوظهور شدیم

به سر پیاده نمودیم طرح انتحاری را
به فکر و راه رسیدن برای حور شدیم

۳۲

وقتی که خسته‌ام، تو برایم سخن مگو
از بوسه و تبسم و چاک یخن مگو

وقتی دلم هوای گل و بوستان نداشت
از یاس و از شقایق و از یاسمن مگو

با یوسفِ ز قافله از یاد رفته‌یی
از خوف و رعب صخره و دشت و دمن مگو

وقتی به پیش حضرت یعقوب می‌روی-
از گرگ و از دریدن و از پیرهن مگو

لطفاً توان و صبر مرا امتحان مکن
از بغض و آه و گریه‌ی هر بیوه زن مگو

وقتی که خود به دور خودم پیچ می‌خورم
از حال زار خسته‌ی هر هم‌وطن مگو

با مادر شکسته‌دل و درد دیده‌ای
از انتحار و توته‌ی عضو بدن مگو

با همسری که منتظر یک بشارت است
با او تو از شهادت و خون و کفن مگو

وقتی ز آب دیده تمام بدن تر است
از ابر و رعد و ریزش باران به من مگو

آنگه تنم که طعمه‌ی یک انفجار شد
از گوشت پاره‌ها تو به آن قبرکن مگو

۳۳

باید مسیر باد صبا را عوض کنیم
باید هوای دهکده‌ها را عوض کنیم

فریادها میان گلو کشته می‌شوند
باید نوای حنجره‌ها را عوض کنیم

با نعره‌های خفته به‌جایی نمی‌رسیم
باید ز بیخ و ریشه صدا را عوض کنیم

دارو دگر نتیجه ندارد به زخم‌مان
فکری به‌هم نموده، دوا را عوض کنیم

باید مسیرِ فیلم به جایِ دگر رود
لازم اگر شود که نما را عوض کنیم

این‌جا هوای دهکده سرد است، بعد از این
باید مسیر صاعقه‌ها را عوض کنیم

با این عصای دست، به مقصد نمی‌رسیم
باید ز دست خویش عصا را عوض کنیم

دستت بده به دست من، آغوش باز کن
مشتی شویم و تا که بلا را عوض کنیم

۳۴

می‌خواستم عصای تو باشم، ولی نشد
یک‌لحظه خاک پای تو باشم، ولی نشد

مادر! نشد که دَین خودم را ادا کنم
هر درد را دوای تو باشم، ولی نشد

مادر! مرا ببخش که در کشتیِ حیات
هرلحظه ناخدای تو باشم، ولی نشد

می‌خواستم به سایه‌ی مهر و محبتت
فرزند باحیای تو باشم، ولی نشد

دانسته‌ام که جای من اندر بهشت نیست
چون سر به گام‌های تو باشم، ولی نشد

مادر! به من تو شیر سپیدت حلال کن
اولاد با وفای تو باشم، ولی نشد

تنها امید و خواهشت این بود، مادرم!
آیینه‌ای نمای تو باشم، ولی نشد

می‌خواستی به قامت خم گشته‌ات، مدام
اِستاده چون رسای تو باشم، ولی نشد

هاونِ روزگار چنان کوفت بر سرم-
دیگر من هم‌صدای تو باشم، ولی نشد

مادر! ببخش چون‌که من از دستِ روزگار
یک لحظه‌ای فدای تو باشم، ولیَ نشد

مادر! ببین که من به چه حد ناتوان شدم
حتی که در هوای تو باشم، ولی نشد

مادر! بیا دوباره به من فرصتی بده
می‌خواستم عصای تو باشم، ولی نشد!

۳۵

کجاست آن‌که به هر پافتاده‌یی عصا ببرد
پیام عاطفه بر نسل بی‌نوا ببرد

کجاست آن‌که به هر شاخه‌های کاج بلند
هوای نغمه به مرغان خوش صدا ببرد

به خاک خفته و از پا فتاده سربازی
به زخم تازه‌ی او کیست تا دوا ببرد؟

میان جاده نشستم که یار نا خَلفی ـ
مرا به حاشیه راند، به انزوا ببرد

ز پا فتاده‌ام اندر میان جاده، مگر
کسی بیاید و ما را به انتها ببرد

به‌سان قایق سرگشته در تلاطم آب
صدای ضجه‌ای ما را به ناخدا ببرد

میان جاده و در انتظار حادثه‌ام
که پاره‌های تنم هر سو در هوا ببرد

۳۶

این‌جا اگر که سر بکشی کشته می‌شوی
حتی زرِه به بر بکشی کشته می‌شوی

باید عمل کنی به پلانی که داده‌اند
گر نقشه‌ی دگر بکشی کشته می‌شوی

دروازه را به روی تو دیوار کرده‌اند
روزی اگر که در بکشی کشته می‌شوی

مثل کبوتری به قفس گیر کرده‌یی
یعنی که بال و پر بکشی کشته می‌شوی

باید درون بُت‌کده‌ی آذری شوی
باری اگر تبر بکشی کشته می‌شوی

این‌جا صدا میان گلو گیر کرده است
محضی اگر خبر بکشی کشته می‌شوی

۳۷

غزنه و بلخ و بدخشان و سرپُل خونین
فاریاب و کنر و لوگر و کابلِ خونین

آسمانِ وطن از ابر سیه پوشیده
پیکرِ خفته و بی‌حالت زابل خونین

صحنه خالی و هوا دود، فضا آلوده
تن سرباز وطن بین قراول خونین

لاله خون است که در سینه‌ی خود جا دارد
مریم و یاسمن سوسن و سنبُل خونین

باغ زخمی و زمین خسته و گل افسرده
شاخه و برگ و تن هر بته‌ی گل خونین

خون هر هم‌وطنم روی خیابانِ جاری
صورت و مویِ پرآشفته و کاکل خونین

۳۸

ای فتنه‌ی زمانه و ای دوره‌ی جنون
ای قرن ظلم و وحشت و ای عصر سرنگون

فرمانروای مطلق و خودکامه‌ی زمان!
بس کن فریب و حقه بدون چرا و چون

از نخوت و غرور تو آتش گرفته‌ایم
زین بیش و بیش‌تر غم ما را مکن فزون

از بهر سرنگونی‌اش ای مادری وطن!
یک آه پر ز غصه کن از سینه‌ات برون

ما مردمان تشنه و در خون تپیده‌ایم
ما کشته می شویم ز دست سیاسیون

ای مرغِ پر شکسته! سلام مرا ببر
بر وادیِ خشونت و جغرافیای خون

۳۹

قلب شکسته و دل ویران چه می شود
قول و قرار و وعده و پیمان چه می شود؟

سوگند خورده بودی و بشکستی اش، مگر
بحث خدا و حرمت قرآن چه می شود؟

حالا که سبزه ی دل ما خشک گشته است
ابر بهاری و قطره ی باران چه می شود؟

در سفره ام نشسته و نان و نمک شدیم
حالا که پاس نان و نمک دان چه می شود؟

با پای خود به خانه ی ما آمدی، ولی —
حالا که قصه ی بز و چوپان چه می شود

عمری ست از پی تو به ابهام می رویم
این کار پشت پرده و پنهان چه می شود؟

کار تو برخلاف تمامی وعده هاست
سازی مرا ز وعده پشیمان چه می شود

گیریم آشنایی ما ختم گشته است
جنگ و جدال و دست و گریبان چه می شود؟

۴۰

در شهر ما دیوانه و هُشیار می‌خندد
در خانه و در حومه‌ی بازار می‌خندد

دیوانه در دنیای خود غرق است، می‌خندد
هوشیار آخر بر کجای کار می‌خندد

شهری‌که در هرجاده‌اش یک لاشه‌ی قتل است
دنیا به حال ملت بی‌مار می‌خندد

شهری که در صد متری‌اش یک جای امنی نیست
دولت برای سرخط اخبار می‌خندد

جایی‌که یک عمری‌ست من مشغول تدریسم
پوهاندها برحال پوهنیار می‌خندد!

هرجا و در هرگوشه‌یی، هرکس به حالِ خود
در کوچه و در جاده‌ی هم‌وار می‌خندد

این‌جا دلیل خنده‌ها را کس نمی‌داند
مأمور در حرف مدیر، اجبار می‌خندد

گه خواب و گه بیدار، گه اِستاده، مستانه
تکرار، هی تکرار، هی تکرار... می‌خندد

۴۱

بنگر چه‌گونه بی‌سر و بی پا و تن شدیم
بی‌خانمان و دربه‌در و بی‌وطن شدیم

با دهُل هرکه آمد و هی پا به پا زدیم
ما حرف ناشنیده درونِ لجن شدیم

با هرکسی رفیق شدیم، مار شد به ما
ما خود هنوز زنده، درونِ کفن شدیم

ما در قمار زندگی این‌گونه باختیم
حتی که لخت و عاری و بی‌پیرهن شدیم

شاید در این معامله ما خود ملامتیم
با سیل اشک، راهیِ دشت و دمن شدیم

دردم نمی‌کند که چه بودیم و چون شدیم
دزد و عیاش و صاحب اموال و زن شدیم

۴۲

آفتاب از آسمان کشورم دزدیده‌اند
خواب را هرشب ز چشم مادرم دزدیده‌اند

مرغ بی‌بالم که راه آشیان گم کرده‌ام
از فراز کاج‌ها بال و پرم دزدیده‌اند

من دراین ویرانه‌ها یک‌لحظه راحت نیستم
آخر از جانِ خودم پیراهنم دزدیده‌اند

از چه‌گویم، با که‌گویم، از کجاها سرکنم
کودکم را روز روشن از درم دزدیده‌اند

سر میان زانویش بنهاده، در فکر خود است
خنده‌ها را از لبان خواهرم دزدیده‌اند

من دگر روی کدامین شانه‌ها باور کنم
تکیه‌گاه و اعتماد و باورم دزدیده‌اند

قصه‌ی تنهایی‌ام را با که من قسمت کنم
هم‌نشین و همدم و هم‌سنگرم دزدیده‌اند

۴۳

هر لحظه نقد ـ نقد، کمی راه حل بگو
راه حلی به قاعده‌ای مبتذل بگو

از طرح و از تئوری و برنامه‌ها چه سود
در ساحه پا گذار و دمی از عمل بگو

از برج‌های سرد زمستان مگو به من
از روزهای تازه و برج حمل بگو

دامن مزن به شعله‌ی تبعیض و اختلاف
راهی بدیلِ آتش و جنگ و جدل بگو

دیری‌ست طعم زهر هلاهل چشیده‌ام
از قند و از شیرینی و طعم عسل بگو

از قله‌ی خیال، به یک شرط بهر من ـ
در پهلویم نشین و برایم غزل بگو

از دوره‌های شاد جوانی و تازه‌گی
افسانه و حکایت و ضرب‌المثل بگو

۴۴

سخت است در این جامعه یک رنگ بمانیم
هم‌رنگِ همین جامعه‌ی لنگ بمانیم

سخت است در این جامعه ما گُم شده باشیم
بی‌عرضُه‌تر و بی‌فر و بی‌هنگ بمانیم

صد رنگیِ ما، بس‌که سبب گشته در این شهر
در فتنه و در شورش و در جنگ بمانیم

سنگی که فقط ظاهر آن رنگ بگیرد
سخت است که ما در دل آن سنگ بمانیم

هرلحظه فقط رنگ عوض می‌شود، این‌جا
این است که بی‌حرمت و بی‌ننگ بمانیم

۴۵

به یاد عاصی بزرگ

عاصی! ببین که خون تو نادیده می‌شود
سنگی به روی قبر تو کوبیده می‌شود

عاصی هنوز زخم وجود تو تازه است
پرونده‌ی ترور تو پوشیده می‌شود

بنگر که باز فتنه رهِ آمدن گرفت
این‌گونه قاتلان تو بخشیده می‌شود

عاصی! تو نیستی که ببینی چه حالت است
اوضاع این زمانه چه پیچیده می‌شود

با خون تو معامله صورت گرفته است
دستان قاتلان تو بوسیده می‌شود

سوداگران که خون شما را فروختند
از چهره‌های این همه فهمید می‌شود

عاصی! در این معامله تنها تو نیستی
خون هزار مثل تو بلعیده می‌شود

۴۶

من و این خاطر ویرانه و این حسِ غریب
من و این زندگیِ لعنتی و رنجِ مهیَب

غصّه و درد و پریشانی و این تنهایی
منِ آواره و شوریده و دنیای عجیب

همه بیمار و پلاسیده و افتاده به خاک
پس در این شهر پر از درد یکی نیست طبیب

ای دل! این خواهش و این عذر و تمنای تو چیست
از خوشی‌های جهان بر تو مگر نیست نصیب

سرنوشت تو به یک توته یخی بسته شده
چون که در یک قدمی های تو مرگ است قریب

۴۷

امشب بسان موسم پاییز خسته‌ام
پاییز خسته از من و من نیز خسته‌ام

بی‌مهریِ زمانه دلم را گرفته است
از خود، از او، خلاصه ز هرچیز خسته‌ام

از بس که صبر و حوصله‌ام سر رسیده است ـ
از قصه‌های فلسفه‌آمیز خسته‌ام

خاموش شد صدای نکیسا و مروَزی
از داستان خسرو و پرویز خسته‌ام

شیرین ز عشق خسرو و خسرو ز عشق او
من هم ز سوز و ناله‌ی شبدیز خسته‌ام

سر تا به پا وجود مرا غم گرفته است
هی پشت هم، پیاپی و یک‌ریز خسته‌ام

امشب ز شور و هلهله خوابم نمی‌برد
از ناله‌های مرغ سحرخیز خسته‌ام

۴۸

بغچه‌ای از سرگذشت و خاطرات آورده‌ام
یک سبد لب‌خند از شهر هرات آورده‌ام

از جلال آباد هم عطر گل نارنج را
بهر تو از کندهار آب حیات آورده‌ام

کشمش از غزنی برایت تحفه، توت از پنجشیر
یک کمی از شهر مولانا نبات آورده‌ام

از سیامو و جلالی، از ضحاک و رابعه ـ
قصه‌ی شهمامه را با جزییات آورده‌ام

بی‌گمان ما را برادرها به چاه انداختند
نردبان عشق را بهر نجات آورده‌ام

قصه‌ها دارم من از هرگوشه‌ی این سرزمین
بوی عشق از چارسوی سرحدات آورده‌ام

هموطن! بگذار دستت را به روی دست من
راه حل از بهر صلح و از ثبات آورده‌ام

گریه را بس کن، برایت تحفه دارم هموطن!
خنده را از بهر دفع مشکلات آورده‌ام

۴۹

چه‌قدر عاجز و درمانده و زبون گشتیم
گنه نکرده و هر روز غرق خون گشتیم

برای این‌که به معراج همدلی برسیم
چه‌قدر کوچک و پامال و سرنگون گشتیم

اگرچه لانه‌ی‌مان روی برگ یک کاج است
مگر چه شد که به این سمت رهنمون گشتیم

ز روی کینه به درهای خویش کوبیدیم
و مثل خانه‌ی بی‌سقف و بی‌ستون گشتیم

به یُمن خوب، در این راه و جاده پا ماندیم
چرا؟ چه شد مگر این‌قدر بدشگون گشتیم

۵۰

زخم ناسور مرا بگذار تا درمان شود
خانه‌ام ویران نمودی، خانه‌ات ویران شود!

خانه‌ات ویران که باغ و خانه‌ام آتش زدی
حیرتم، آدم چرا این‌قدر بی وجدان شود؟

مثل بلخ و اندراب از چشم من خون می‌چکد
حالت پنجشیر را نگذار گورستان شود

دشت بکوایم، ببین حال مرا خشکیده‌ام
آب شو تا لاله روید سنبل و ریحان شود

نه قناعت می‌دهد نه هم قناعت می‌کند
از خر شیطان مگر این‌روزها پایان شود!

خانه‌ام سرد و خُنَک، حالم زمستان گشته است
روزها در انتظارم تا که تابستان شود

آسمان! لطفی بکن باران بیاور، سوختم
ابر شو، بگذار این‌جا یک‌کمی باران شود

۵۱

از پشت قله‌های جهان سر برآورید
با فکر ناب و طرح کلان سر برآورید

در عمق آسمان بِدرید ابر تیره را
مثل غرور یک خَلَبان سر برآورید

گرگان کمین گرفته و هی زوزه می‌کشند
مانند یک غرور شبان سر برآورید

پولاد بشکنید و رهی جست‌وجو کنید
مانند رودبار روان سر برآورید

با نعره‌ی بلند، جهان را تکان دهید
با قدرت و غرور و توان سر برآورید

راه‌های رو به‌پیش و عقب بسته‌اند، پس
پیدا نموده ره، ز میان سر برآورید

جرمی نکرده‌اید و چرا کشته می‌شوید؟
بهر حراست تن و جان سر برآورید

راه علاج درد، فقط در تقابل است
بهر مهار این سرطان سر برآورید!

۵۲

شاخه بشکستند، باغ و لانه را آتش زدند
شمع را کشتند شب، پروانه را آتش زدند

دست یازیدند بر تاریخ و بر فرهنگ ما
داستان و قصه و افسانه را آتش زدند

در پی نابودیِ ما آستین را بر زدند
دفتر و دیوان و قصر و خانه را آتش زدند

دست و پای ما به دستور اجانب بسته شد
با کدامین جرم این کاشانه را آتش زدند؟

هیچ‌کس از ظلم و استبدادشان باقی نماند
آرزوی عاشقِ دیوانه را آتش زدند

یک‌به‌یک چادر به‌سر کردند رهبرهای ما
اعتماد و باورِ مردانه را آتش زدند

من دگر روی کدامین شانه‌ها باور کنم
بر گلو بردند تیغی، شانه را آتش زدند

درد کابل نیست، این درد بزرگ پارسی‌ست
از هریوا رفته تا فرغانه را آتش زدند

۵۳

افتادی و گفتم چه شد؟ افگار شدی؟ نه!
زین بخت فلاکت‌زده بی‌زار شدی؟ نه!

عمری پی آموزش و تحصیل دویدی
آخر چه؟ مگر صاحب یک کار شدی؟، نه!

با قافیه‌ها می‌روی هرلحظه کلنجار
پس صاحب یک دفتر اشعار شدی؟، نه!

چشمک زدی و آینه انداختی از دور
بر دختر هم‌سایه گرفتار شدی؟ نه!

دیوانه به دیوانگی‌اش خوش‌ِگِل و زیباست
از صحبت عاقل مگر هُشیار شدی؟ نه!

دیدی همه‌ی گوشه و اطراف جهان را
از حادثه آگاه و خبردار شدی؟ نه!

بخت آمد و بر گوش من آهسته چنین گفت:
از خواب گران یک‌شبه بیدار شدی؟ نه!

تقدیر ز من می‌کند هرلحظه سؤالی
افتادی و برخواستی، افگار شدی؟ نه!

۵۴

هرچه عاجل‌تر از این شهر سفر باید کرد
قصد یک دهکده و شهر دگر باید کرد

آزر از بُت‌گری‌اش دست نبرداشته است
زود برخیز و فقط فکر تبر باید کرد

روز و شب بر سر ما شام سیه می‌گذرد
شب ماتم‌زده را زود سحر باید کرد

مردم هرلحظه فقط منتظر شلاق‌اند
دیگر از حاکم این شهر حذر باید کرد

ای‌دل! این شهر پر از درد دگر جای تو نیست
تا به کی پیرهنِ غصه به بر باید کرد

هم‌سفر! قصه‌ی این فاجعه از یاد ببر
حرفی از هجرت ناخواسته سر باید کرد

۵۵

مرا به بوم و بری این کرانه دفن کنید
مرا به رسم سیاه زمانه دفن کنید

مرا به آب هریرود و غزنه غسل دهید
به خاک میهن من، بی‌بهانه دفن کنید

مرا به دامن پامیر و بلخ و هندوکش
به خاک میهن من، عاشقانه دفن کنید

به‌وقت مردن من آه و ناله سر ندهید
مرا به ساز غزل، شاعرانه دفن کنید

مرا به زیر درختان توت قریه‌ی من -
به‌زیر سایه‌ی دیوار خانه دفن کنید

برای این‌که برایم دعای‌تان برسد
مرا به قریه‌ی زیبای «آستانه» دفن کنید

مرا به دامن این خاک خسته بسپارید
بدون گریه، فقط محرمانه دفن کنید

مسافران خسته نبینند پیکر من را
مرا به‌خاک، ز سوی شبانه دفن کنید

به روی سنگ مزارم به گریه بنویسید:
«غریب و بی‌وطنم» عاجزانه دفن کنید!

۵۶

یک پنجره باز است، دگر پنجره بسته
یک قلب پر از عشق، دگر قلب شکسته

گه روزنه تاریک، گهی روزنه روشن
گه با دل آرام، گهی با دل خسته

عمری‌ست به یک جاده‌ی تاریک و پر از خوف
گه صف به صف هستیم، گهی رسته به رسته

با قایق بشکسته روانیم به هر موج
گاهی تک و تنها و گهی دسته به دسته

در خانه‌ی دل در زدم ای عشق! کجایی؟
گفتند که در ماتمِ تقدیر نشسته!

۵۷

شکوفه داشت گل؛ اما بهار خالی بود
و باغ‌ها همه‌جا از چنار خالی بود

درخت‌ها همه‌سو سبز و بارور بودند
درخت سیب مریض و انار خالی بود

فضای دهکده مثل همیش مهتابی
کنار پنجره، شب جای یار خالی بود

به دوش هریک‌شان کوزه، از پی آب ـ
میان این‌همه جایِ نگار خالی بود

به سوی دره همه یک ردیف می‌رفتند
لبانِ تشنه، ولی رودبار خالی بود

هوای قریه برایم نداشت آرامش
دگر ز قیمت و از اعتبار خالی بود

درخت دهکده را زود با تبر کشتند
و سایه‌اش همه از انتظار خالی بود

مسافران همه از نیمه‌راه برگشتند
سفر دراز، ولی کوله‌بار خالی بود

مسافری که به هرسو غریب می‌دیدم
نشسته بودم و اما کنار خالی بود

۵۸

باز هم خون و باز هم تقبیح، باز هم حرف‌های تکراری
باز هم اشک و ناله و حسرت، باز هم آه و گریه و زاری

باز هم مادری به سوگ پسر، باز هم خواهری نشسته به خاک
مادرم! عرض تسلیت دارم، باز صبر و دوباره دل‌داری

باز هم بر کناره‌ی دیوار، یادگاری ز خون سرخ پسر
باز بنشسته در گلیم عزا، باز در سوگ و در عزاداری

باز آژیر آمبولانس هرسو، باز پشت در شفاخانه
باز بیرون نمودنِ تابوت، باز هم لحظَه‌های دشواری

باز هرسو جنازه و تدفین، باز هم کشته‌های نامعلوم
خون سرخ هزار هم‌وطنم، باز در روی جاده‌ها جاری

۵۹

مادر! ببین چه‌گونه تنم را دریده‌اند
کفتارها چه‌سان یخنم را دریده‌اند

مادر! بیا ببین پسرت در چه حالت است
از شستِ پای، تا دهنم را دریده‌اند

یعقوب نیست واقف از احوال یوسفش
گرگان مصر پیرهنم را دریده‌اند

مادر! بیا تو با نخ و سوزن کنار من
عاجل بدوز، چون کفنم را دریده‌اند

فرصت نشد که راحت و آسوده‌جان کنم
حتی‌که دست و پا زدنم را دریده‌اند

هرشام کز نیامدنم گفت کودکم
آخر به او بگو بدنم را دریده‌اند

مادر! میانِ غلغله تنها نسوختم
احساس می‌کنم وطنم را دریده‌اند

۶۰

شب‌های زرد و زار دگر عادتم شده
این وضع ناقرار دگر عادتم شده

لب‌ریز گشت کاسه‌ی صبر و امید من
چشمان انتظار دگر عادتم شده

این‌جا صدای ضَجه به‌گوشم نمی‌رسد
بی‌رحمیِ عیار، دگر عادتم شده

هرجا صدای ناله و فریاد و ماتم است
باروت و انفجار دگر عادتم شده

ترسی ز زخم و سوز مغیلان نباشدم
تأثیر دردِ خار دگر عادتم شده

بختم سیاه و قسمت و تقدیر من خراب
این‌حال و روزگار دگر عادتم شده

از بس‌که زهر تلخ ز دشمن چشیده‌ام
شوربای زهرمار دگر عادتم شده

۶۱

فطرت آزاده می‌خواهم خراسانم برید
اصفهان و غور و یزد و تاجیکستانم برید

مشهد و پامیر و بلخ و سُغد و کابل خانه‌ام
مرو می‌خواهد مرا، باری سمنگانم برید

هستی‌ام، روح و روانم، جسم و جانم؛ پارسی‌ست
بهر جان بخشیدنش کولاب و تهرانم برید

از تبار جامی و خیام و البیرونی‌ام
بر مزار حضرت ناصر بدخشانم برید

هم‌زبان و هم‌نژاد و کیش و آیینیم ما
شهر طوس و وخش و فرخار و شبرغانم برید

ای سمرقند! ای بخارا! ای تمام هستی‌ام!
از برای هم‌دلی بر شهر ختلانم برید

لندن و پاریس و مسکو کی شود خاک هری
دره‌ی پنجشیر و ورزاب و خُزستانم برید

کاسه‌ی صبرم به سر شد در دیار بی‌کسی
میله‌ی گل‌تپه و سالنگ و پغمانم برید

خواهشم از دوستان این است بعد از مُردنم-
از برای دفن کردن در «کرامانم» برید

۶۲

فطرتم، عشقم ، تمام هست و بودم؛ پارسی‌ست
هستی‌ام، روح و روانم، تار و پودم؛ پارسی‌ست

سجده‌گاهم بلخ، تسبیح و ثنایم مثنوی
پیشوایم حافظ و جامی، درودم؛ پارسی‌ست

مکتبم اقبال و بیدل، درس من فردوسی است
تکیه‌گاهم حضرت سعدی وجودم؛ پارسی‌ست

زادگاهم مرو، تهران و دوشنبه خانه‌ام
لهجه‌ام دُرِ دری، گفت‌وشنودم؛ پارسیست

رهنمایم بوعلی، تاریخ من شهنامه است
لحن و صوت و چامه و نظم و سرودم؛ پارسیست

هفت اورنگش غرورم، افتخارم گنجوی
ماه و روز و صبح و شام و دیر و زودم؛ پارسیست

بوی جوی مولیانش را ز نای و نی شنو
تار و تنبور و رباب و چنگ و عودم؛ پارسی‌ست

۶۳

با احمق و هُشیار، بلد می‌شوم آخر
در کوچه و بازار، بلد می‌شوم آخر

یک‌روز دیگر بیش در این شهر بمانم
با پودر و سیگار، بلد می‌شوم آخر

با خواهر بی‌چاره و این حالت حیران
با مادر بیمار، بلد می‌شوم آخر

بیزارم من از آتش و از اسلحه؛ اما
با مرد کمان‌دار، بلد می‌شوم آخر

از حالت و اوضاع وطن یافتم امروز
با سرمه و دستار، بلد می‌شوم آخر

حیرانم من از دولت بی‌ماهیت؛ اما
با این سِر و اسرار، بلد می‌شوم آخر

هرچند که پرورده‌ی از آتش و دودم
با شهر عزادار، بلد می‌شوم آخر

آهنگ سفر دارم از این شهر پر از غم
با مردم اغیار، بلد می‌شوم آخر

من می‌روم از کشور و تا زنده بمانم
کم‌کم به همه کار، بلد می‌شوم آخر

من نسل ستم‌دیده و منفور زمانم
با وضع رقت‌بار، بلد می‌شوم آخر

حلّاجم و اسرار همی فاش بگویم
با چوب سرِ دار، بلد می شوم آخر

Contributors

Fazel Ahad Ahadi holds a bachelor's degree in cinema and theater from Kabul University and a master's degree in cultural studies from the University of Mirza Torsonzadah in Dushanbe. From 2005 to 2021 he was a professor in the Faculty of Arts, Kabul University, where he was active in many cultural and administrative bodies. He was a visiting professor in the Department of Cinema and Media Studies at the University of Chicago in 2021-24.

A prolific writer, Ahadi has published a dozen books and half a dozen journal articles in Persian, one book and two articles in Cyrillic, and one journal article in English. Among these works are a collection of short stories, many plays or film scripts, and seven collections of poetry. None of these works has been translated into English, but two individual poems have been. "I'm Antigone" and "Silent City" were published in the program for the University of Chicago's Court Theatre production of *Antigone* (www.courttheatre.org/wp-content/uploads/2024/01/Antigone-Program-January-2024.pdf).

This collection of poems, *I Am the Wounded Victim of a Suicide Bomber*, was originally published in Persian as *Man jesm-e zakhm-khorde-ye yek entehari am* (I am the wounded victim of a suicide bomber) in Afghanistan in 2023, but banned shortly after. These poems draw heavily from the recent history of Afghanistan, torn apart by years of warfare and subject to domination by outsiders and extremist groups. The struggles of Afghanis to keep alive their individual and collective identities under such trying conditions are highlighted in the collection. While a few of the poems are joyful and hopeful, most evoke the pain and suffering of separation and isolation, mixed with the determination to endure, persist, and resist.

Pouneh Shabani-Jadidi is Instructional Professor of Persian at the University of Chicago. She received a PhD in Linguistics from the University of Ottawa in 2012 and an earlier one in Applied Linguistics with a focus on translation from Tehran Azad University in 2004. She is the author of *Processing Compound Verbs in Persian: A Psycholinguistic Approach to Complex Predicates* (2014) and *Translation Metacognitive Strategies* (2009). In addition, she is the editor of *The Routledge Handbook of Second Language Acquisition and Pedagogy of Persian* (2020) and co-editor of *The Oxford Handbook of Persian Linguistics* (2018), *The Routledge Handbook of Persian Literary Translation* (2022), and *The Art of Teaching Persian Literature: From Theory to Practice* (Brill 2024). She has co-translated several books from Persian into English with Patricia J. Higgins, namely *The Thousand Families: Commentary on Leading Political Figures of Nineteenth Century Iran* (Peter Lang 2018), *Hafez in Love: A Novel* (Syracuse University Press 2021), *Island of Bewilderment: A Novel of Modern Iran* (Syracuse University Press 2022), and *The Bewildered Cameleer: A Novel of Modern Iran* (Mazda Publishers 2023). In addition, she has co-translated Sohrab Sepehri's poetry collection, with Prashant Keshavmurthy, as *The Eight Books: A Complete English Translation* (Brill 2021, 2024).

Patricia J. Higgins is University Distinguished Service Professor Emerita at SUNY Plattsburgh. She received a PhD in anthropology from the University of California, Berkeley in 1974 and taught courses in anthropology and women's studies, primarily at SUNY Plattsburgh, from 1973 until her retirement in 2011. In addition to an eighteen-month ethnographic study of education and socialization in Tehran, she spent ten months as a Fulbright Lecturer at Tehran University and later conducted ethnographic research with Iranian-origin parents and students in Santa Clara County, California. Her work has been published in *Iranian Studies*, *NWSA Journal*, *Signs*, *Human Organization*, and *Practicing Anthropology* and as chapters in several edited volumes. She also served as editor of *Practicing Anthropology*, monograph series editor for the Society for Applied Anthropology, and co-editor of the books, *Classics of Practicing Anthropology: 1978–1998* and *The Routledge Handbook of Persian Literary Translation*. She is co-translator, with Pouneh Shabani-Jadidi, of *The Thousand Families: Commentary on Leading Political Figures of Nineteenth Century Iran* by Ali Shabani, *Island of Bewilderment*: A *Novel of Modern Iran* by Simin Daneshvar, *The Bewildered Cameleer* by Simin Daneshvar, and *Hafez in Love: A Novel* by Iraj Pezeshkzad, which was awarded the 2021 Lois Roth Persian Translation Prize.

Nile Green is Professor of History and the Ibn Khaldun Endowed Chair in World History at the University of California, Los Angeles. He holds an MPhil in Middle Eastern studies from Cambridge and a PhD from London University's School of Oriental and African Studies and has traveled extensively in the Middle East and South Asia, including Afghanistan. His study of the multiple globalizations of Islam and Muslims has resulted in a dozen books, including *Global Islam: A Very Short Introduction* (Oxford, 2020), *Terrains of Exchange: Religious Economies of Global Islam* (Oxford 2015), and *The Love of Strangers: What Six Muslim Students Learned in Jane Austen's London* (Princeton, 2016), and in additional edited collections, including *The Persianate World: The Frontiers of a Eurasian Lingua Franca* (UC Press 2019) and *Afghan History Through Afghan Eyes* (Oxford, 2015). Reviews of his books have appeared in *The New York Times* (as Editors' Choice), *The New Yorker, The New York Review of Books, The Los Angeles Review of Books,* and *The Times Literary Supplement*, as well as in major newspapers across the English-speaking and in South Asia and the Middle East. He has also published dozens of articles in such journals as *Afghanistan, Iranian Studies, Journal of Asian Studies, International Journal of Middle East Studies*, and *Comparative Studies in Society and History,* and in edited volumes.